The Power Of Godly Purpose

By
Bishop Femi Owoyemi

1

The Power of Godly Purpose

Copyright @ 2023 by Bishop Femi Owoyemi

ISBN: 978-7332330-6-4

Scripture quotations are taken from the Holy Bible: New King James Version - NKJV and the King James Version - KJV.

Bishop Femi Owoyemi
P. O. Box 41235
Providence, RI 02940. USA.

DEDICATION
This book is dedicated to the glory of the Almighty, the worker of miracles, signs, and wonders, who transforms lives and brings hope in hopeless situations. I dedicate this book to Him who has wisdom, power, and might to fulfill His purpose. He made Abraham fruitful at the age of 100 and caused the 90-year-old womb of Sarah to bring forth. To Him alone be all the glory forever and ever. Amen.

ACKNOWLEDGEMENT
I am grateful for the tremendous contribution of my family in the journey of faith. Their steadfastness and sacrifices gave me the strength to trust and rely absolutely on God long enough to experience the benefits of His faithfulness.

I acknowledge the contributions of Professor E. C. Osondu. God used him to revive the publishing ministry. He is always available to review and edit the manuscripts despite his busy schedule. May the good Lord bless him, his work, and his family in Jesus' name. Amen.

Bob and Linda Padgett greatly blessed us. They also introduced us to the printer of our books. Bob went to be with the Lord in May 2023. We greatly miss him. May the Lord strengthen and renew Linda and the family in the name of Jesus Christ.

I also thank our daughter Favour, whose gift of grace is a great blessing to the family, church, and the publishing ministry. She designs the front and back covers of our books. May the Lord richly bless her in the mighty name of Jesus Christ.

And we know that all things work together
for good to them that love God,
to them who are the called according to his purpose.
Romans 8:28.

TABLE OF CONTENTS

Chapter One

ABOUT THIS BOOK

This is the third book in the series on the *Purpose of God.* The first was *Understanding the Purpose of God,* and the second was *Knowing and Fulfilling the Purpose of God.* This third book, *The Power of Purpose,* is written to show the tremendous power available in Christ to those who desire to fulfill the purpose of God. Romans 11:33-34 says, *"O the depth of the riches both of the wisdom and knowledge of God! how unsearchable are his judgments, and his ways past finding out! For who hath known the mind of the Lord? or who hath been his counsellor?"* The wisdom of God is unsearchable. God, through His works, reveals His ways to help us understand how to relate to Him, fulfill His purpose, and live a fulfilled life. He displayed His awesome ingenuity by aligning purpose and creation. It is wise to be in alignment with God. The lives of those who devote themselves to the purpose for which God created them confirm this.

This book aims to explore the alignment of creation and purpose to reveal the multi-dimensional benefits available to those who engage in the purpose of God. It is written to show the amazing grace that is available to those who commit to God's purpose. The purpose of God is the key to God's treasury of resources and grace. This book will illuminate the divine privileges that God extends to empower those who choose to fulfill His purpose. It will examine some of the unlimited grace available to those who desire to fulfill the purpose of God. It is these divine privileges or grace that we describe as 'The Power of Purpose.' This power is available to every believer who chooses to fulfill the purpose of God. The objective of this book is to motivate you to accept and engage in the plan of God for your life and to fulfill it by spotlighting this powerful phenomenon.

This book presents the amazing and life-transforming benefits available to those who engage in the purpose of God. The assignment for which God created you is the purpose of God for your life. It is what He wants you to do. It is not what you choose for yourself.

By enumerating some of the amazing grace available to you, this book seeks to inspire you to embrace and pursue the purpose that God has for your life. God's omnipotence and omniscience are available to you if you embrace His purpose. You will receive all things you need for life and godliness through the knowledge of Him who has called you to glory and virtue - 2 Peter 1:3. Engaging in the purpose of God is what will bring you the contentment, peace, and joy that you seek in life.

- If you desire to be fulfilled;
- If you desire to live with contentment;
- If you desire to have peace;
- If you desire to be relevant;
- If you desire to make your life count;
- If you desire to make an impact;
- If you desire to leave a legacy;
- If you want to influence people yet unborn;
- If you want earthly and heavenly rewards, you must locate and fulfill the purpose for which God created you.

Chapter Two

THE NATURE OF PURPOSE

Some of the benefits of living for a purpose or cause are:
- Self-motivation and enthusiasm.
- Absence of boredom and aimlessness.
- Productive engagement of time and resources.
- Diligence, tenacity, and determination.
- Thoroughness, effectiveness, and confidence.
- Tangible output, outcomes, impact, and results.
- Satisfaction and accomplishment.

People tirelessly seek relevance, blessings, peace, joy, and fulfillment. Contentment is not guaranteed in all good or productive activity. Great philanthropists may still lack peace and fulfillment. After accomplishing the good plans they set for themselves, people still feel empty because relevance, blessings, peace, joy, and fulfillment are not found in self-appointed ventures but in the pursuit of the purpose of God. People still feel empty, frustrated, and unfulfilled even after they have accomplished great things, but this is not the experience of those engaged in the purpose of God.

The Purpose Of God Is Eternal

Creative works are products of a purpose designed to benefit someone or something. Purpose is the mother of creation. It must precede creation or invention because it is the reason for creating or inventing. There is nothing on earth or in heaven that is older than the purpose of God. God's purpose is eternal - Ephesians 3:11. It is the reason for creation. Creation was designed to fulfill the purpose of God. Since it is made by the only wise, omniscient, omnipotent, and omnipresent God, it must function as it was designed to. Since God designed creation to fulfill

His purpose, that purpose must endure. It cannot fail. It cannot be modified, and it cannot be abandoned. Since the purpose of God is eternal in its origin, it must endure in its operation, and it must control all divine activities throughout eternity. Creation can never fulfill any other purpose. Therefore, it is foolish for anyone to be involved in anything that is contrary to the purpose of God.

Purpose Determines Action
Purpose determines action. The nature of a person shapes his or her intent. It is unusual for people to act contrary to their desires. A person's nature is determined by his or her core values. Greedy people are exploitative because of their greed. Selfish values produce selfish purposes that are selfishly promoted. A good and beneficial purpose must foster the common good. God created man and endowed him with good core values to fulfill a good purpose. God gave man righteousness, love, justice, and peace in the beginning. These are the core values of God. They were to foster life and peace (Malachi 2:5). When man sinned, his core values were contaminated. Since the purpose of God can only be fulfilled through His core values, God must reinstate His core values in us through the Holy Spirit in order to accomplish the good that He purposed for His kingdom and for us.

Nothing Has Meaning Without Purpose
"I have seen all the works that are done under the sun; and, behold, all is vanity and vexation of spirit. That which is crooked cannot be made straight: and that which is wanting cannot be numbered. I communed with mine own heart, saying, Lo, I am come to great estate, and have gotten more wisdom than all they that have been before me in Jerusalem: yea, my heart had great experience of wisdom and knowledge. And I gave

9

my heart to know wisdom, and to know madness and folly: I perceived that this also is vexation of spirit. For in much wisdom is much grief: and he that increaseth knowledge increaseth sorrow." Ecclesiastes 1:14-18. Without purpose, life is meaningless. Our life has no meaning if there is no purpose to it. The value of life is in the purpose it serves. That purpose is designed by God. God created us for a good purpose - Ephesians 2:10. He works with us to fulfill His good purpose - 2 Timothy 3:16-17; Titus 2:14; 3:8; Hebrews 10:24. Purpose gives meaning to everything. Our life has meaning when it is devoted to the good purpose of God. We are fulfilled when we live for the purpose of God. The purpose of God is good. No one is fulfilled doing bad things because God did not create us to do bad things. *"For we are his workmanship, created in Christ Jesus unto good works, which God hath before ordained that we should walk in them." Ephesians 2:10.* Pursuing your own desires is selfish and will result in aimlessness, frustration, and torment. If you live outside the purpose of God, you will eventually realize that your life is lived for vanity.

Failure to embrace the purpose for which God created us is the source of human suffering. There is limited progress in the world because we seek power for selfish purposes. Good purpose brings progress. Progress is a product of good purpose that is well executed. If we do what is good, there will be progress. If the world embraces the purpose of God, great things will be accomplished. People's lives will be better, and we will be fulfilled by bringing good to others. Living without embracing the purpose of God results in a wasted life.

Purpose And Functionality
Products are made to fulfill a specific purpose. A product that is well made will fulfill the purpose for which it is

10

made. A product's intended performance must dictate its design. There must be harmony of intent, design, fabrication, and operation. Purpose and functionality must be aligned in a product. There is disequilibrium when things are out of order, and disharmony cannot produce peace. There is no perfect alignment of purpose and functionality outside the purpose of God. Fulfilling the purpose of God is what will fulfill you. No one can have peace outside the purpose of God because there cannot be peace between God and a person who rejects His purpose. Think about it. All things work as they are designed to. A bicycle cannot be a motorcycle, and a car cannot work like a truck. A truck cannot be a train, and a helicopter cannot function as an airplane. Created things work according to how they are made. The animals created to live in water will perish on land. You know that this is the truth. This is the principle that governs all lives, including yours. Your life will be meaningless and empty if you reject the purpose for which God made you. Stubbornly doing your own thing will only bring you confusion and stagnation. Continuously seeking the peace, blessings, fulfillment, and joy, which are accessible only in the purpose of God from elsewhere, is foolish. Embracing the assignment for which God created you will terminate your frustration, strife, emptiness, hopelessness, and depression. If you devote yourself to the purpose of God, you will be fulfilled.

Purpose Is Non-negotiable
The purpose of God was determined before He created all things. What is created cannot alter the purpose for which it is created. Things made cannot alter the purpose for which they are made but must work to fulfill the purpose for which they are made. This is the nature of all created and man-made things. For example, computers, phones,

motor vehicles, furniture, cooking utensils, etc. do not alter the purpose for which they are made. They submit to the authority of their maker and function to fulfill his purpose, desire, will, and intent. A product that is made perfect does what it is made to do. Therefore, what is made does not have the power to alter, change, or modify the purpose for which it was made. Since man did not negotiate his purpose with God, he cannot renegotiate, change, or alter it. The only sensible thing a man can do is accept and fulfill the purpose for which God made him.

The Purpose Of God Is Immutable
Purpose can be short-term or long-term. Whether short-term or long-term, purpose is specific and to accomplish it, discipline and endurance are imperative. God does not change. His purpose has not changed. His wisdom does not change. He knows all things. There is nothing new for Him to learn. So, everything that He does must fulfill His eternal purpose. The eternal purpose of God is to build Himself a kingdom on earth. God created all things for this purpose. It is the reason for which God created you and me. The Scriptures say that God made man in His own image and according to His own likeness. Male and female, He made them. His purpose was that man would fill and have dominion on the earth, to manage and administer it. That purpose has not changed and has not been altered. The purpose God has for all things and all of us has not changed - Genesis 1:26-28; 2:1-25. In Jesus Christ, God will establish and administer His kingdom on earth and rule among His citizens (believers). A foretaste of the Kingdom of God is revealed in the lives of mature believers now. Though it will be shown in the Millennial Reign of Christ - Revelation 20:4, its full manifestation will be in the eternal reign of Jesus Christ - 1 Corinthians 15:22-28; Revelation 21:1-4. From Genesis to Revelation,

God continues to intimate us with that purpose and how He will accomplish it. Nothing can stop His purpose.

Rejecting The Purpose Of God Is Sin
Sin is any act contrary to the word and intent of God. Sin is refusing to be who God wants you to be. Sin is rejecting the place and responsibility God assigned to you. Sin is devising and pursuing a plan contrary to God's desire for your life. Sin is refusing to live as God intends. Sin is of the devil, who is its originator - 1 John 3:8. Any act contrary to the word of God sets us against Him. It makes us rebellious and sinful. Those who indulge in sin cannot be fulfilled in life. God created Lucifer, that great dragon, the serpent of old, called the Devil and Satan, as an archangel. He created him to minister on the holy mountain of God - Ezekiel 28:11-14. Satan, choosing to be and to do something else, rebelled against God - Ezekiel 28:15 and Isaiah 14:12-14. He started a war in heaven, did not prevail, and was cast out - Revelation 12:1-12.

God created Adam and Eve to rule on earth under His authority - Genesis 1:26-27; 2:1-28. Satan, in order to oppose the purpose of God, cajoled them to disobey God, thereby causing their fall - Genesis 3:1-24; Romans 3:23; 5:12-14. Having fallen, mankind was unable to fulfill the purpose of God. Satan usurped their authority, subjugated them, and began to rule the earth - Romans 6:16; 2 Peter 2:19; Matthew 4:8-9; 12:26; Luke 4:6. Satan is the god of this world who blinds people to the gospel - 2 Corinthians 4:4. He is the prince and ruler of this world - John 12:32; 14:30; 16:11. He is the prince of the power of the air and the spirit that works in the children of disobedience - Ephesians 2:2. The world under his influence is full of wickedness - 1 John 5:19. He controls all human beings who do not believe in Jesus Christ - Ephesians 2:1-3;

13

4:17-19. By acting contrary to the purpose of God, Satan, demons, and human beings can never be fulfilled.

Redemption And Deliverance Precede Restoration
No one can fulfill the purpose of God in the kingdom of Satan. Being an enemy of God, he tirelessly frustrates those in bondage under him so that they cannot fulfill the purpose of God. If the purpose of God is to be fulfilled as intended, man must be delivered from the power and dominion of Satan. He must be set free. Jesus Christ came for this reason.

Adam and Eve had dominion on earth before the fall. They had fellowship with God in the Garden of Eden - Genesis 3:8. When they disobeyed God, they acquired a sinful nature. Satan, whom they obeyed, gained dominion over them. Being subject to him, they lost their authority and ability to maintain dominion on earth. By His death on the cross, Jesus Christ destroyed the dominion of Satan over man. When you receive Jesus Christ as Savior and Lord - John 3:3-5, you are delivered from the kingdom of Satan, transferred into the kingdom of God - Colossians 1:12-13, and positioned to fulfill His purpose.

Saved, Reconciled, And Restored To Fulfill Purpose
If a product works contrary to the purpose for which it is made, it is faulty. Producers are responsible for restoring products that malfunction. A manufacturer's warranty is often offered for this purpose. We know that God (the Producer) created man (the product) to have dominion on earth and, through obedience, fulfill His purpose (function). Man sinned (malfunctioned) when he disobeyed God. Sin made man faulty and incapable of fulfilling the purpose for which God created him. Since a product that functions contrary to the intent for which it is made is imperfect, God needed to correct the imperfection

in man so that he can fulfill the purpose for which he is made.

To do this, God, in Jesus Christ, took responsibility and became man - John 1:14. He died on the Cross to make atonement for sins - 1 John 2:2; John 3:16. He offered forgiveness and salvation to all - 1 John 4:10; Hebrews 2:14; Philippians 2:5-8. Those who receive Him and believe in His name are saved and reconciled to God - Colossians 1:21; 2 Corinthians 5:17-21; Romans 5:10. He gives them the Holy Spirit to teach and empower them to fulfill the original purpose for which He created them - 1 Corinthians 3:16; 6:19; John 14:26; Acts 1:8.

Human beings are created to fulfill the original intention of God. This original intention is the eternal purpose which God purposed in Christ. In Christ, all believers are reconciled to God to fulfill the purpose of God. Those who reject Jesus Christ unwittingly reject their restoration and exempt themselves from the plan of God. Generally, people who reject the purpose of God live frustrated and empty lives. They are frustrated because they turn from the purpose of God to another purpose, which they do not have the ability to fulfill. They feel empty and unfulfilled. Proverbs 16:4a says, *"The Lord hath made all things for himself."* Colossians 1:15 also says, *"For by Him all things were created that are in heaven and that are on earth, visible and invisible, whether thrones or dominions or principalities or powers. All things were created through Him and for Him."* God made all things for Himself. He made us for Himself. We must agree with the purpose for which He made us. We must return to the original intent of God. We cannot function as we ought to outside of God's original plan. Just as producers design products with the ability and capacity to fulfill the intent for which they are made, so it is with us. We have been made to fulfill the intent of our Creator. We have been packaged for that purpose. You are designed to fulfill the purpose for which God created you. You do not have the ability to do what God did not create you to do. If you turn from the purpose of God to another thing, you cannot succeed, and you will be frustrated because you are saved, restored, and reconciled to fulfill the purpose of God.

Your Impact Is In The Purpose Of God
How a thing is made limits its ability to do what it is not designed for. God designed us to administer the world. We can only do so according to the intent, the blueprint, the manual, the will, the word, and the counsel of God, who made us. That we have our own will does not make us independent of our Maker. We should humbly exercise our will to fulfill the purpose of God - Proverbs 3:5; 16:25; Jeremiah 10:23; Psalm 37:23. To accomplish the great things that God desires for us, we must embrace the purpose of God. Turning from that purpose is pride and causes God to resist us - James 4:6. No one is more knowledgeable, powerful, or wiser than God. We must surrender to His purpose because we cannot be fulfilled in anything apart from the purpose for which God created us. Fame, wealth, and power are no substitutes for the peace and fulfillment that is in the purpose of God.

Chapter Three

DIVINE PURPOSE AND GRACE

"Wherefore I put thee in remembrance that thou stir up the gift of God, which is in thee by the putting on of my hands. For God hath not given us the spirit of fear; but of power, and of love, and of a sound mind. Be not thou therefore ashamed of the testimony of our Lord, nor of me his prisoner: but be thou partaker of the afflictions of the gospel according to the power of God; Who hath saved us, and called us with an holy calling, not according to our works, but according to his own purpose and grace, which was given us in Christ Jesus before the world began, but is now made manifest by the appearing of our Saviour Jesus Christ, who hath abolished death, and hath brought life and immortality to light through the gospel:" 2 Timothy 1:6-10.

Called To The Purpose Of God

Every human being is called to receive salvation. They are also called to the purpose of God. Salvation is the gateway to the purpose that God wants us to fulfill. Like Timothy, we are saved and called with a holy calling. God called us to fulfill a purpose. He has an assignment that He wants us to fulfill while we are here on earth. He called us because of His purpose and grace. Grace refers to the gifts that God gives to fulfill His purpose. The Apostle Paul told Timothy not to be afraid but boldly to use the gift of God that was in him. Romans 12:6 also says that we should use the gifts that God has given us to fulfill His purpose. In eternity past, God purposed to save mankind through Jesus Christ, not because of any deserving act but by grace. Understanding this will help us willingly embrace any affliction or suffering in our quest to fulfill the purpose of God, knowing that He will help us accomplish it.

God does nothing without purpose. Nothing just happens. God called us for a reason. Thinking that salvation is the only objective of God for us is incorrect. In addition, He has ministries that He wants us to fulfill. He saved us to serve. He has a vested interest in all aspects of the assignment He gives us. He is committed to His purpose. He will work with us as He worked with the Lord Jesus Christ. As He activated His grace to fulfill His purpose in our salvation, He will do the same by giving us the grace we need to fulfill His purpose. Purpose and grace are complements, and it is the theme of this book. God does not just do things; He does things to advance His purpose. A God-given grace empowers us to fulfill our purpose.

God created mankind in His own image and according to His likeness to rule on Earth. We are individually unique. God uniquely equipped us to fulfill His purpose. He has given us the wisdom, knowledge, understanding, and authority we need to do so. These are examples of the grace in us to fulfill the purpose of God. No other creature has any competence comparable to man. God created you for a purpose. He did not create you for mere existence. When you engage in the purpose of God, things will work supernaturally in your life. The power of God is available to you to accomplish the will of God.

The story of Timothy typifies the story of all human beings. The purpose of God for him preceded his birth, conversion, and encounter with Paul. God gave Timothy the gift he needed to fulfill His plan. It was that gift that the Apostle Paul encouraged him to stir up and use for God. This is the procedure that God follows with every human being. God's plan or purpose for us precedes our birth and conversion. To fulfill His purpose, God gives us the gifts we need. In principle, grace must be released to fulfill the purpose of God. Everyone who is willing to fulfill the purpose of God cannot lack the grace he or she needs. Our responsibility is to identify and use the gift that God has given us to fulfill His purpose. No one can fulfill the purpose of God without the gift of grace. Grace is the enabling power for fulfilling purpose.

The power of purpose is the grace that God dispenses to and on behalf of those who commit to fulfilling His purpose. The power of purpose is the divine operation set in motion by God to advance and fulfill His purpose through man. Paul told Timothy to recognize that God gave him the Spirit of power, love, and a sound mind. These are examples of the grace available to all believers who want to fulfill the purpose of God. Through the Holy Spirit, a believer has access to the power he needs to fulfill the purpose of God. Love will be shed abroad in his heart for the things of God - Romans 5:5. He will not be confused but will be equipped with a sound mind for his assignment. The Holy Spirit will direct his work through the wisdom of God to accomplish his assigned task.

God called all of us according to His purpose and grace. Purpose and grace work together. Grace is not only operational in our salvation or calling but also in the purpose that God wants us to fulfill. In other words, grace cannot be withheld from or denied to those who want to fulfill the purpose of God. In addition, God did not call us to fulfill His purpose on our own. It is not possible to fulfill the purpose of God in our strength. Zechariah 4:6 says, *"So he answered and said to me: "This is the word of the LORD to Zerubbabel: Not by might nor by power, but by My Spirit,' says the LORD of hosts."* God's purpose can only be fulfilled by recognizing and engaging the grace that God gives. God faithfully supplies the grace we need to accomplish His desire, be it character, wisdom, knowledge, understanding, disposition, power, resources, connections, favor, etc. This is a great blessing for those who live for God. They never lack grace for impact. Our fulfillment in life is predicated on engaging in the purpose of God using the grace He has given to us.

Divine Positioning

Divine positioning is an act of grace that is crucial for fostering our ability to fulfill the purpose of God. God constantly uses situations, circumstances, associations, events, and other means to put us in the position that will help us recognize, acknowledge, embrace, and fulfill the purpose He has for our lives. Isaiah 45:21 says that God is just. Acts 7:52; 22:14; Romans 3:26; Zechariah 9:9, and 1 Peter 3:18 confirm this. So, God justly positions us to fulfill His purpose by the operation of His grace. Those who devote themselves to the purpose of God enjoy privileges that others do not. God works in them, with them, for them, and through them to fulfill His purpose. Since no man knows the whole counsel of God, no one can position himself to fulfill the purpose of God. We need the help of God to be in the position where we will fulfill His purpose. Some of the things that God does and uses to position us include the following:

1. Birth

By birth, God positions us on Earth to fulfill His purpose. God put John in Israel by birth to be the forerunner of Jesus Christ - Luke 1:13-17 and John 1:23. Jesus Christ was born a Jew, in the tribe of Judah, to the house of David, to fulfill His promise to Abraham - Genesis 12:1-3, Judah - Genesis 49:8-12, and David - 2 Samuel 7:1-17. Acts 17:26-28 says that God determines the time and place of our birth to put us in a position to fulfill His purpose. The nation, state, town or city, and family of our birth shape our ability to fulfill the purpose of God.

2. Restoring Our Relationship With God

The most important divine positioning act is the restoration of the relationship between God and man. After the fall of man, only redemption and reconciliation could enable mankind to fulfill the purpose of God. For this reason, God had to deal with the issue of sin since *"All have sinned and fall short of the glory of God"* - Romans 3:23. Sin separated man from God, His purpose, mercy, goodness, and help - Isaiah 59:2. Scriptures affirm that the sinner must suffer the penalty for sin - Deuteronomy 24:16, 2 Chronicles 25:4, and Ezekiel 18:20. Blood is required to atone for sins - Hebrews 9:22. The blood of atonement must be pure, but sin has corrupted the blood of Adam, Eve, and their offspring. The polluted blood of the sinner cannot atone for sins. Since a bad tree cannot bear good fruit - Matthew 7:18, Adam and Eve were in no position to produce a sinless offspring to atone for their sins. For this reason, God temporarily used animal sacrifice to atone for the sin of Adam and Eve - Genesis 3:21. He later codified this into Law - Leviticus 17:11. Unfortunately, the blood of bulls and goats cannot take away sin - Hebrews 10:4. If the blood of animals and of man cannot atone for sins, the only option for God was to become man, live a sinless life, and become the sacrifice of atonement.

Consequently, God, in Isaiah 7:14, announced that a virgin shall be with child. By the power of the Holy Spirit, God caused Mary, a virgin, to conceive Christ - Luke 1:26-37. Jesus Christ, God the Word - John 1:1-3, became flesh - John 1:14. He is the seed of the woman that was promised in Genesis 3:15. He received a body in the womb of Mary to make atonement for sins - Hebrews

21

10:5-14. After Mary gave birth to Him - Matthew 1:18-21, He finished His ministry, went to the Cross, bruised the head of Satan, the serpent - Genesis 3:15, destroyed his works - 1 John 3:8, and defeated him - Hebrews 2:14-15. Those who believe in Him are delivered from the powers of darkness - Colossians 1:13. Reconciled to God - 2 Corinthians 5:18-21, they are brought into a position to fulfill the eternal purpose which God purposed in Christ before the foundation of the world - Ephesians 3:11.

God can do all things, and no thought of His heart can be frustrated - Job 42:2. With God, all things are possible - Matthew 19:26 and Mark 10:27. Jesus Christ, the grace of God, is the source of salvation and reconciliation. God restores relationships with anyone who believes in Jesus Christ and puts them in a position to fulfill His purpose. Jesus Christ is the sacrifice of atonement. His blood has washed away your sins. Reconciliation with God is the door to discovering and fulfilling the purpose of God. You need to be reconciled to God by faith in Jesus Christ so that you can be positioned to fulfill the purpose of God for your life. Repent now and ask the Lord Jesus Christ to forgive you and save your soul so that you can fulfill His purpose for your life.

3. Deliverance From The Power Of Sin
By delivering us from the stronghold of sin, God puts us in a position to fulfill His purpose. Anyone under sin is incapable of fulfilling the purpose of God. In addition to delivering us from the kingdom of darkness, God must deliver us from the power of sin if we are to fulfill His purpose. When Adam and Eve sinned, they developed a sinful nature. The sinful nature rebels against the will of God. It kills the desire for godly service and makes it impossible to fulfill godly purpose - Romans 8:5-8. No sinful person can fulfill the purpose of God. Through

22

Christ, God delivered us from the power and dominion of sin to fulfill His purpose - Romans 6:3-14. With His blood, Jesus Christ washed away our sins - 1 John 1:7, Romans 5:18-19, Ephesians 1:7, and 2 Corinthians 5.21. He dwells in us by His Spirit - 1 Corinthians 3:16 and 6:19-20 so that we can receive the desire and strength to fulfill His purpose. Through the Holy Spirit, He makes us will and do according to His good pleasure.

Romans 6:8-13 says, *"Now if we died with Christ, we believe that we shall also live with Him, knowing that Christ, having been raised from the dead, dies no more. Death no longer has dominion over Him. For the death that He died, He died to sin once for all; but the life that He lives, He lives to God. Likewise you also, reckon yourselves to be dead indeed to sin, but alive to God in Christ Jesus our Lord. Therefore do not let sin reign in your mortal body, that you should obey it in its lusts. And do not present your members as instruments of unrighteousness to sin, but present yourselves to God as being alive from the dead, and your members as instruments of righteousness to God."* In Christ, we died to sin, and as He lives for God, so must we, because we have been made instruments of righteousness unto God.

Sin frustrates our ability to fulfill the purpose of God. 1 John 3:8-9 says, *"He who sins is of the devil, for the devil has sinned from the beginning. For this purpose the Son of God was manifested, that He might destroy the works of the devil. Whoever has been born of God does not sin, for His seed remains in him; and he cannot sin, because he has been born of God."* The Holy Spirit empowers us to overcome sin. He keeps us holy - Romans 1:4. He uses the word of God, which is the truth, to transform and renew our minds - Romans 12:1-3, cleanse us - John 15:3, sanctify us - John 17:17, and give us faith - Romans 10:17, to fulfill God's purpose.

4. Deliverance From Lust

Satan promotes covetousness, which engulfs the mind and arouses desires for riches, power, and fame. These desires breed greed, callousness, and wickedness. The lust of the eyes, the lust of the flesh, and the pride of life distract us from fulfilling the purpose of God. God delivers us from these things through His word and the power of the Holy Spirit. Galatians 5:16 says that if we walk in the Spirit, we will not fulfill the lust of the flesh. Colossians 3:1-3 urges us to set our affection on things above and not on the things on earth. 1 John 2:15-17 also instructs that we should not love the world or the things in the world. James 4:4 says that a person who is a friend of the world is an enemy of God. Titus 2:12 admonishes that, denying ungodliness and worldly lust, we should live soberly, righteously, and godly in this present age. By receiving and practicing these godly instructions, we are delivered from lust and empowered to fulfill the purpose of God because we cannot fulfill the purpose of God if we are in bondage to lust.

To fulfill the purpose of God and be fruitful, we must give up selfish ambition. Romans 12:1 says, *"I beseech you therefore, brethren, by the mercies of God, that you present your bodies a living sacrifice, holy, acceptable to God, which is your reasonable service."* Presenting our bodies as a living sacrifice to God destroys personal and selfish ambition. Jesus said that we must lose our lives for His sake - Matthew 16:25. Unless a kernel of wheat falls to the ground and dies, it remains alone, but if it dies, it brings forth fruit - John 12:24-25. To deliver us from selfish ambition and barrenness, Jesus Christ appoints apostles, prophets, evangelists, pastors, and teachers -

24

Ephesians 4:11-15 - to train and strengthen us for the work of ministry. We must discipline our bodies and put them in subjection - 1 Corinthians 9:27, like the Apostle Paul, so that we can fulfill the purpose of God.

5. Deliverance From The Love Of Money

God delivers us from the love of money when we allow the Holy Spirit and the Word of God to work in us. The love of money is the root of all evil. It is the cause of greed, wickedness, pride, and selfishness. It is responsible for most of the terrible disasters in the world. It is the cause of economic injustice. 1 Timothy 6:9-10 says, ***"But those who desire to be rich fall into temptation and a snare, and into many foolish and harmful lusts which drown men in destruction and perdition. For the love of money is a root of all kinds of evil, for which some have strayed from the faith in their greediness, and pierced themselves through with many sorrows."*** The love of money is idolatry, and it turns people's hearts from God. For the love of money, people take advantage of the poor. They forget that they brought nothing into the world and will take nothing out of it - 1 Timothy 6:7. Whatever we have, we first received - 1 Corinthians 4:7. As stewards of God, we must use our resources for His glory - Matthew 24:14-51. Selfishly acquiring wealth at the expense of the poor will attract the judgment of God - James 5:1-6; Jeremiah 17:9-11. The love of money destroys ministry. Meditating on the Word and practicing it will deliver us and put us in a position to fulfill God's purpose - Matthew 6:19-21; 6:25-34; Luke 16:10-13. Everywhere in the world, it is glaring that wickedness is increasing because of the love of money. Life matters very little to many people. People's desire for comfort and affluence blinds them to the value of life and the needs of others. This must change because all ministry is to enhance life.

25

6. Deliverance From Pride

God created us in His image and likeness to fulfill His purpose and endowed us with what we need to do so. That purpose is to have dominion on earth. Every gift of grace given by God is to serve His purpose. Through sin, ignorance, and pride, people arrogantly and selfishly use divine grace to oppress others. The love of money makes them adopt selfish policies that impoverish, subjugate, and enslave people created in the image and likeness of God. The Holy Spirit, through the word of God, delivers us from pride to position us to fulfill the purpose of God.

Romans 3:10-18 describes the general disposition of all human beings, saying, *"As it is written: "There is none righteous, no, not one; There is none who understands; there is none who seeks after God. They have all turned aside; they have together become unprofitable; there is none who does good, no, not one." "Their throat is an open tomb; with their tongues they have practiced deceit"; "The poison of asps is under their lips"; "whose mouth is full of cursing and bitterness." "Their feet are swift to shed blood; destruction and misery are in their ways; and the way of peace they have not known." "There is no fear of God before their eyes."* People who engage in unrighteousness unwittingly hinder the purpose of God and consequently become incapable of fulfilling it. Righteousness and justice equip us to avoid ungodly acts, thereby enabling us to fulfill God's purpose.

7. Deliverance From Superiority Complex

Historically, mankind, being ignorant of the purpose of God, oppressed and enslaved one another. Ignorance and pride, which make people feel superior, cause them to oppress and deny others their liberty. It is impossible for the oppressor or the oppressed to fulfill the purpose of God. This is a double tragedy. It is a satanic attack on the

26

kingdom of God. By oppressing others, the oppressor prevents the oppressed from fulfilling the purpose of God. Consequently, by preventing others from fulfilling the purpose of God, he likewise cannot fulfill the purpose of God. Genesis 1:26 says that God made human beings in His own image and according to His likeness to have dominion on earth. Acts 17:26 says, from one blood, God made all nations of men. God also said that all men have sinned and fall short of the glory of God - Romans 3:23. If they are made from one blood, and they have all sinned, and they have all fallen short of the glory of God, then they are all the same. No one is superior to another.

Erroneously thinking that they are inferior, Adolf Hitler, in the second world war, destroyed millions of Jews. Millions of Africans were enslaved and killed because, like Hitler, Arabs and Europeans think that Africans are inferior. Romans 12:3 says, *"For I say, through the grace given unto me, to every man that is among you, not to think of himself more highly than he ought to think; but to think soberly, according as God hath dealt to every man the measure of faith."* Thinking you are superior to others is thinking more highly than you ought to think of yourself. That is exactly what Satan did and lost his position, making it impossible for him to fulfill the purpose that God created him to fulfill.

Through discrimination, many are still being denied the opportunity to fulfill the purpose of God. God created everyone to have dominion on earth. A person under oppression cannot have dominion. Oppressing others is contrary to the will of God. By His example and teaching, Jesus Christ revealed the nature of God, to show us how to conduct ourselves. God anointed Jesus Christ to deliver mankind from Satan – the oppressor. He delivered those who are oppressed by the devil - Acts 10:38 - because oppression frustrates the purpose of God.

Superiority complex is of the flesh. God does not support it. Galatians 6:3 says, *"If anyone thinks himself to be something, when he is nothing, he deceives himself."* Thinking that one race is superior to another is deceiving, and it promotes insensitivity, cruelty, and injustice. A superiority complex and pride are the causes of the slave trade, colonization, and economic exploitation. God made mankind in His own image. No one is superior. Slavery, oppressive economic policies, exploitation, and racism subvert the purpose of God. They must be discouraged and eradicated.

Jesus Christ said that we should love our neighbor as ourselves - Matthew 22:39. Love promotes what is good for others, thereby fulfilling the purpose of God. Luke 6:31 says, *"And just as you want men to do to you, you also do to them likewise."* Taking advantage of others, using our strength to oppress others, and denying them the good things of life cannot fulfill the purpose of God. Philippians 2:4 says, *"Let each of you look out not only for his own interests, but also for the interests of others."* We must avoid selfishness and greed. We must treat others as we expect them to treat us. As members of the same body with different and unique abilities, we should use our gifts to edify one another - Romans 12:4-8.

1 Corinthians 4:7 says, *"For who makes you differ from another? And what do you have that you did not receive? Now if you did indeed receive it, why do you boast as if you had not received it?"* We are recipients and stewards of the grace of God. God did not give us grace to oppress but to bless mankind. Arrogance and ignorance produce abuse, but humility and knowledge empower us to fulfill

28

the purpose of God. If we repent and obey the word of God, we will be delivered from these grave errors. Our minds will be renewed, and we will fulfill the purpose for which God created us. If we arrogantly continue to oppose the purpose of God by taking advantage of others, God's judgment is inevitable - Galatians 6:7-8.

God equips us with humility, understanding, and wisdom. We should not be puffed up but, by humility, embrace and practice the wisdom of God. James 4:6-10 says, *"But He gives more grace. Therefore He says: "God resists the proud, but gives grace to the humble." Therefore submit to God. Resist the devil and he will flee from you. Draw near to God and He will draw near to you. Cleanse your hands, you sinners; and purify your hearts, you double-minded. Lament and mourn and weep! Let your laughter be turned to mourning and your joy to gloom. Humble yourselves in the sight of the Lord, and He will lift you up."* By renewing our minds, cleaning our hearts, abandoning pride, and turning from cruelty to others, we are empowered to fulfill the purpose of God.

8. Deliverance From Inferiority Complex

Divine power is available to deliver those who desire to fulfill the purpose of God from an inferiority complex. An inferiority complex is a barrier to fulfilling the purpose of God. Though we may feel incompetent, God makes us competent to fulfill His purpose - 2 Corinthians 3:5-6. Feeling inferior to someone else destroys confidence. Ask God to fill you with the Holy Spirit. Acts 4:13 says, *"Now when they saw the boldness of Peter and John, and perceived that they were uneducated and untrained men, they marveled. And they realized that they had been with Jesus."* Verse 31 said, *"And when they had prayed, the place where they were assembled together was shaken; and they were all filled with the Holy Spirit, and they*

29

spoke the word of God with boldness." The Holy Spirit gives us confidence and boldness to express the grace of God in us without feeling inferior to anyone.

You should never feel inferior. You are made in the image and likeness of God. You are what God says you are. You are fearfully and wonderfully made - Psalm 139:14. You are the work of God, and the work of God is perfect - Deuteronomy 32:4. You are perfect. Your race, skin, and size are perfect. God has loaded you with the gifts He wants you to use for His purpose. You are unique, and so is your gift. Do not be intimidated. Confidently use your gift for the glory of God. This is how you fulfill the purpose of God. Lift up your head. Ignore the negative things that others say and believe what God says about you. Man is mostly wrong because he is limited in knowledge, understanding, and wisdom. God, who is all wise, all knowing, and who understands all things, cannot be wrong. Believe and rely on His word. Step out in faith and let Him use you. He created you to fulfill His purpose. Trust Him. Follow the principles in His word and the voice of the Holy Spirit. God is with you like a mighty warrior, and He will work with you.

9. Deliverance From Limitations
Limitations undermine the ability to fulfill the purpose of God. God delivers those oppressed by the devil, heals the sick, removes curses, and destroys bondage. He delivers people from spiritual, physical, emotional, and mental limitations so that they can fulfill the purpose for which He created them. Luke 1:68-75 says, *"Blessed is the Lord God of Israel, for He has visited and redeemed His people, and has raised up a horn of salvation for us in the house of His servant David, as He spoke by the mouth of His holy prophets, who have been since the world began, that we should be saved from our enemies*
30

and from the hand of all who hate us, to perform the mercy promised to our fathers and to remember His holy covenant, the oath which He swore to our father Abraham: To grant us that we, being delivered from the hand of our enemies, might serve Him without fear, in holiness and righteousness before Him all the days of our life." Jesus Christ came to deliver mankind from limitations. He is the sacrifice of atonement. By His death on the cross, He delivered us from captivity and bondage to Satan, so as to put us in a position to fulfill the purpose of God. To appropriate what He has done, you must receive Him as your Savior and Lord. If you reject Him, you cannot fulfill the purpose of God or escape the eternal consequences of sin. Deliverance is paramount for divine positioning to fulfill the purpose of God.

10. Relocation And Repositioning

God positions us by relocation. For example, in Genesis 37, God, in two dreams, revealed His purpose to Joseph. Joseph related the dreams to Jacob, his father, and his brothers. His brothers, because of envy, hated him and determined to sabotage his dream. In Genesis 37:12-17, Jacob sent Joseph to his brothers, who had gone to feed the flock in Shechem, to "go and see if it is well" with them and with the flock. He inquired from a man who told him that his brothers had gone to Dothan. Joseph found them at Dothan, but when he got to them, they bound him and sold him to the Ishmaelites. In Genesis 39, the Ishmaelites brought Joseph to Egypt and sold him to Potiphar. Joseph served his master faithfully until his master's wife falsely accused him of attempted rape, and he was thrown into prison. In Genesis 40, Pharaoh put his cupbearer and baker in the same prison where Joseph was. The cupbearer and the baker had dreams that Joseph correctly interpreted for them. Two years later, in Genesis

31

41, Pharaoh had a dream that he did not understand, and no one could interpret it. The Cup Bearer remembered Joseph and told Pharaoh about him. Joseph was released from prison, and he interpreted Pharaoh's dream. Being impressed, Pharaoh immediately appointed Joseph the Prime Minister and gave him the authority to manage the economy of Egypt. Joseph built grain reserves in the first seven years of good harvests. In Genesis 42, at the time of famine, Joseph's brothers came to Egypt to buy grain but did not recognize him. On their return trip to Egypt in Genesis 45, Joseph revealed himself to his brothers. To shield his family from the famine, Joseph invited his father, brothers, and their families to Egypt. It is worthy of note that from the time Joseph went to look for his brothers, in obedience to his father, God used the injustices he suffered to bring him to the position where he fulfilled the purpose of God - Genesis 45:7-8. In the same way that God relocated Joseph to the place where he would fulfill his destiny, He still uses the events of our lives to place us where we will fulfill His purpose.

In 1 Samuel chapter 9, Saul, accompanied by a servant, obediently went to look for his father's lost donkeys. They went from one place to another but did not find the donkeys. Eventually, they got to a city where they decided to consult a seer who might guide them to where they could find the donkeys. They met some young men and asked for the seer. The young men answered, *"there he is, just ahead of you. Hurry now; for today he came to this city, you will surely find him before he goes up to the high place to eat. As soon as you come into the city, you will surely find him before he goes up to the high place to eat. For the people will not eat until he comes, because he must bless the sacrifice; afterward those who are invited will eat. Now therefore, go up, for about this time you will find him."* 1 Samuel 9:12-14. That seer was Samuel. The day before, the Lord told Samuel, *"tomorrow, about this time, I will send you a man from the land of Benjamin, and you shall anoint him commander over my people Israel, that he may save my people from the hand of the Philistines; for I have looked upon my people, because their cry has come to me."* 1 Samuel 9:16. When Samuel saw Saul, the Lord told him, *"there he is, the man of whom I spoke to you."* - 1 Samuel 9:17. Saul, who did not know Samuel, asked him, *"Please tell me, where is the seer's house?"* Samuel answered, *"I am the seer."* He invited Saul to the high place to eat, told him that the donkeys he was looking for were found, and that it has pleased God to anoint him king over Israel. The following day, Samuel anointed Saul, saying, *"Is it not because the LORD hath anointed thee to be captain over his inheritance?"* 1 Samuel 10:1. Saul's obedience to his father and his persistence in finding the lost donkeys were the instruments that God used to lead him to Samuel, who anointed him king of Israel on God's instruction. God will order our steps for an encounter to fulfill His purpose.

In 1 Samuel 17, David, on his father's instructions, took provisions to his brothers who went to war with Saul, the king. David came just in time to see Goliath challenging the army of Israel. By faith in God, he confronted and overcame the bear and lion that endangered his father's flocks. God used David's deliverance to prepare him for the encounter with Goliath. Relying on that experience, David confidently challenged Goliath, killed him, and delivered the army of Israel, thus fulfilling the purpose of God. God still uses events, attacks from the enemy, and undeserved suffering to lead us to the place where we will fulfill the purpose He has for our lives.

God relocated Abraham to Canaan - Genesis 12:1-3. In old age, God empowered him and Sarah to give birth to Isaac - Genesis 21:1-3. It was said, "In Isaac shall your seed be called" - Genesis 21:12. Abraham and Sarah became the father and mother of nations. Through their lineage, Jesus Christ was born, and all the families of the earth are blessed through Him - Genesis 12:3. Their relocation enabled them to fulfill the purpose of God. By grace, God relocated Esther and Mordecai to Medo-Persia. He put Esther in the palace and promoted Mordecai to the most prominent position, next to the king, to save the Jews from their enemies, thereby fulfilling His purpose.

11. The Grace Of God

God positions us to fulfill His purpose by equipping us with unique gifts that make room for us or position us to do so. Joseph's gift of interpreting dreams positioned him to fulfill the purpose of God in Egypt. The same was true of Daniel in Babylon. By grace, God empowered Cyrus to conquer Babylon and touched his heart to free the Jews to build the temple.

God also puts us in a position to fulfill His purpose by shaping our disposition and character to do so. Psalm 78:70-72 says, *"He also chose David His servant, and took him from the sheepfolds; [71] From following the ewes that had young He brought him, to shepherd Jacob His people, and Israel His inheritance. [72] So he shepherded them according to the integrity of his heart, and guided them by the skillfulness of his hands."* God put in David the fear of God so that he could lead Israel with integrity. He was the standard for the kings of Israel.

These works of grace are indicative of God's vested interest in our assignments, and He quietly does them to equip us to successfully accomplish His purpose.

34

Chapter Four

THE HOLY SPIRIT IN THE PURPOSE OF GOD

The power of God available to those who commit to His purpose is multi-dimensional. Whether we are aware of it or not, God logistically orders His power and grace so that His purpose will be accomplished by those He calls.

The Holy Spirit
The Holy Spirit is the most important ally in fulfilling the purpose of God. His primary responsibility is to help the saints live the life that God wants them to live and also to accomplish their assigned responsibilities. The power, wisdom, ability, and desire to fulfill purpose come from the Holy Spirit. He is the administrator of the plan of God on earth. He is the overseer of the estate of God. No one can know or fulfill the purpose of God without the Holy Spirit. He must lead, guide, instruct, and empower us if we are to succeed in our assignment.

However intelligent you are and however great your plan, riches, or connections, you cannot fulfill the purpose of God without the power of God. The power of God is from the Holy Spirit. Zechariah 4:6 says, *"Not by might nor by my power; but by my spirit saith the Lord of hosts."* Psalm 97:1-6 depicts the power of God, saying, *"The LORD reigns; Let the earth rejoice; Let the multitude of isles be glad! Clouds and darkness surround Him; Righteousness and justice are the foundation of His throne. A fire goes before Him and burns up His enemies round about. His lightnings light the world; The earth sees and trembles. The mountains melt like wax at the presence of the LORD, at the presence of the Lord of the whole earth. The heavens declare His righteousness and all the peoples see His glory."* A fire goes before Him and burns up His enemies round about. Divine power gives the believer victory over opposition to divine assignment. The power of God is the antidote to the continuous and unabated assault of the devil on those who want to fulfill the purpose of God. Psalm 62:11 says, *"God has spoken once, twice have I heard this: that power belongs to God."* All power in the universe belongs to God, and He engages it to further His purpose. 1 Corinthians 4:20 says, *"The kingdom of God is not in words but in power."* Without the Holy Spirit, you cannot fulfill the purpose of God for your life. It is through the Holy Spirit that we can do the works that God prepared in advance for us to do.

The Holy Spirit's Work In Jesus Christ

Jesus Christ is the pattern. Acts 10:38 says, *"How God anointed Jesus of Nazareth with the Holy Ghost and with power: who went about doing good, and healing all that were oppressed of the devil; for God was with him."* The power of the Holy Spirit was on the Lord Jesus Christ to do good and to bring relief to those oppressed by the devil. He was born of the Holy Spirit - Luke 1:35. Before commencing His ministry, He was baptized in the Holy Spirit - Matthew 3:16. He was full of the Holy Spirit - John 3:34. He was led by the Holy Spirit to the wilderness to face temptation - Matthew 4:1 and Luke 4:1. He returned in the power of the Holy Spirit - Luke 4:14. He was empowered for ministry by the Holy Spirit - Luke 4:18. He ministered in the power of the Holy Spirit - Matthew 12:28. He was empowered by the Holy Spirit to offer Himself on the cross for our redemption - Hebrews 9:14. He was raised by the power of the Holy Spirit and seated at the right hand of God in heaven - Ephesians 1:19-20. As the Holy Spirit empowered Jesus Christ in all facets of life and ministry, so He empowers everyone who chooses to fulfill the purpose of God.

The Holy Spirit And The Purpose Of God
Just like Jesus Christ, the believer is born of the Holy Spirit - John 3:6-7. John 20:21-23 says, *"Peace be unto you: as my father has sent me, so send I you. And when He had said this, He breathed on them, and said to them, "Receive the Holy Spirit. If you forgive the sins of any, they are forgiven them; if you retain the sins of any, they are retained."* In Luke 24:49, Jesus said, *"And, behold, I send the promise of my Father upon you: but tarry ye in the city of Jerusalem, until ye be endued with power from on high."* In Acts 1:8, He reiterated, *"But you shall receive power when the Holy Spirit has come upon you; and you shall be witnesses to Me in Jerusalem, and in all Judea and Samaria, and to the end of the earth."* Before commencing ministry, the Apostles were baptized in the Holy Spirit. In Acts 2, He sent the promise of the Father - the Holy Spirit - upon them to empower them for their mission - Acts 2:16-18. In Acts 8, 10, and 19 the Lord also baptized believers with the Holy Spirit to empower them for ministry. Jesus still baptizes believers with the Holy Spirit to help them fulfill God's purpose.

At the beginning of my ministry, the Lord told me that *ministry can only be done in the power of the Holy Spirit.* Zechariah 4:6, Isaiah 42:1, and Isaiah 11:1-9 confirm this. Isaiah 61:1-3 says, *"The Spirit of the Lord GOD is upon me; because the LORD hath anointed me to preach good tidings unto the meek; he hath sent me to bind up the brokenhearted, to proclaim liberty to the captives, and the opening of the prison to them that are bound; To proclaim the acceptable year of the LORD, and the day of vengeance of our God; to comfort all that mourn; To appoint unto them that mourn in Zion, to give unto them beauty for ashes, the oil of joy for mourning, the garment of praise for the spirit of heaviness; that they might be called trees of righteousness, the planting of the LORD, that he might be glorified."* God wants believers to reveal His glory. Ephesians 1:12 and 1:14 affirm this. To accomplish this, the gospel must be preached, the depressed must be healed, the captives must be set free, those in bondage must be released, and liberty must be granted to all. These cannot be achieved without the Holy Spirit because the purpose of God will only be accomplished through the power of God.

He Empowers Us For Divine Assignments
The frustration of many servants of God is in relying on themselves rather than on God. Divine assignments cannot be fulfilled in the flesh. Since the assignment is of God, it requires the power of God for its fulfillment. God must empower us to preach the gospel and to carry out every divine assignment - Acts 6:1-8. In John 15:5 He said, *"Without me, ye can do nothing."* Every divine assignment requires the power of the Holy Spirit. It is the Holy Spirit who enables believers to fulfill the purpose of God. The Holy Spirit enabled Bezalel, the son of Uri, to design and fabricate all the items of the tabernacle - Exodus 35:30. In Exodus 31:2-5, God told Moses, *"See, I have called by name Bezalel the son of Uri, the son of Hur, of the tribe of Judah. ³ And I have filled him with the Spirit of God, in wisdom, in understanding, in knowledge, and in all manner of workmanship, ⁴ to design artistic works, to work in gold, in silver, in bronze, ⁵ in cutting jewels for setting, in carving wood, and to work in all manner of workmanship."* It is the Holy Spirit that also equipped him to teach others.

Through the Holy Spirit, God gave Daniel and his friends knowledge and skill in all literature and wisdom; and

38

Daniel had understanding in all visions and dreams - Daniel 1:17. By this, God distinguished them among their peers and all the magicians of Babylon, qualified them for high office in the empire, and they fulfilled His purpose. Through the Holy Spirit, Joseph received the gift of understanding and interpreting dreams, which enabled him to fulfill the purpose of God in Egypt. In one form or another, David, Solomon, Ezekiel, the prophets, and priests were empowered by the Holy Spirit to fulfill the purpose of God. To fulfill their ministries, the Holy Spirit empowered the apostles to preach and perform miracles, signs, and wonders.

Divine assignments are impossible to fulfill in our strength. When we give ourselves to fulfilling the purpose of God, He gives us His own power to do it. The anointing makes a huge difference in the lives of believers. It practically shapes everything we do. It is not available to those who do not devote themselves to the purpose of God. 1 Samuel 2:9 says that by strength shall no man prevail. Jesus Christ said, "Of myself, I can do nothing." - John 5:19 and 5:30. Most people, being unaware of the tremendous advantage in the power of the Holy Spirit, seek to accomplish divine assignments in their own strength. They strategize, plan, and organize to execute the purpose of God without consulting the Holy Spirit. They overburden themselves and become frustrated, even though the amazing power of God is available to them. Romans 4:20 says that the kingdom of God is not in words only but in power. It is the power of God that distinguishes the children of God, and by operating in the wisdom of God, they outwit geniuses.

He Instructs Us
By far, the most beneficial tool for fulfilling the purpose of God is divine instruction. God always instructs those

who embrace His purpose. For example, in the Garden of Eden, He told Adam how he should live - Genesis 2:15-17. Until he violated God's instruction, he lived a life that pleased God. God had fellowship with him daily. His personal relationship with God was by far the most intimate. God visited him in the cool of the day. Until the kingdom of God is established at the return of Jesus Christ, probably no man will be able to have such a quality relationship with God. God instructed Noah on how to build the ark - Genesis 6:13-16. As they continued in His purpose, God instructed the Patriarchs in many ways and at various times.

Beginning from Egypt, through the wilderness, and for forty years, God never failed to instruct Moses and also Joshua in their assignments. It was the Holy Spirit that instructed Bezalel, the son of Uri, on how to design, sculpt, and produce all the objects for the tabernacle - Exodus 31:1-11. God guided Samuel to identify and anoint Saul the king of Israel - 1 Samuel 9:15-17. When Saul failed, God instructed and guided him to anoint David king - 1 Samuel 16:1-12. The Holy Spirit instructed and led Philip to the Ethiopia Eunuch - Acts 8:26-38. He instructed Ananias and led him to minister to Paul - Acts 9:10-20. Peter was led by the Holy Spirit to minister to Cornelius and his household - Acts 10:9-35. The Holy Spirit guided Paul to Macedonia to fulfill the purpose of God - Acts 16:6-40. The Holy Spirit taught Joseph and Daniel to administer the political and economic sectors of great empires. God never fails to guide and instruct those who walk in His purpose. We must expect to be guided in the same manner. It is through instructions from God that we can fulfill His purpose. Romans 8:14 says, *"For as many as are led by the Spirit of God, they are the sons of*

God." Ignoring the voice of the Holy Spirit will destroy our efforts to fulfill the desire of God.

Three things are necessary to appropriate the benefits of divine instructions for fulfilling the purpose of God. The first, which has been illuminated through our discussion so far, is the source. Only instructions from God should be acknowledged and embraced. The second is to keep the purity of the instruction. We must not modify divine instructions because that will jeopardize the assignment. Moses never failed until he struck the rock which God told him to point at - Numbers 20. Saul, the first king of Israel, lost his throne because he did not fully obey the Lord. Lastly, divine instructions must be obeyed if we want to fulfill the purpose of God. Through the guidance of the Holy Spirit, we overcome the ignorance, confusion, distraction, deception, and errors that undermine the purpose of God.

He Empowers Us For Extraordinary Results
1 Corinthians 1:26-29 says, *"For you see your calling, brethren, that not many wise according to the flesh, not many mighty, not many noble, are called. But God has chosen the foolish things of the world to put to shame the wise, and God has chosen the weak things of the world to put to shame the things which are mighty; and the base things of the world and the things which are despised God has chosen, and the things which are not, to bring to nothing the things that are, that no flesh should glory in His presence."* The anointing empowers ordinary people to produce extraordinary results. Those reputed for strength, might, and wisdom in the world are disarmed by anointed servants of God. At the trial of the Apostles, in Acts 4:13 the Bible says, *"Now when they saw the boldness of Peter and John, and perceived that they were uneducated and untrained men, they marveled.*

41

And they realized that they had been with Jesus." The Sanhedrin marveled at the boldness, amazing competence, and intelligence of the Apostles (whom they said were uneducated and untrained.) Being anointed, they could not be intimidated or harassed by religious leaders. God equipped them with His power and wisdom to disarm their opponents and fulfill His purpose.

The anointing is responsible for the feats accomplished by the people of God. In addition, they have access to the wisdom of God because hidden in Jesus Christ are all the treasures of wisdom and knowledge - Colossians 2:3. In Mark 6:2, speaking about Jesus, the people said, *"From whence hath this man these things? And what wisdom is this which is given unto him, that even such mighty works are wrought by his hands?"* To fulfill the purpose of God, divine wisdom is available to procure, organize, and manage resources. The competence of those working on the purpose of God is not theirs; It is from God. In 2 Corinthians 3:5, the Apostle Paul said, *"Not that we are sufficient of ourselves to think any thing as of ourselves; but our sufficiency is of God."* We have the sufficiency and competence through the anointing. In all generations, through the Holy Spirit, God equips His servants with His power and wisdom to accomplish His purpose. It is the Holy Spirit who empowers us to outsmart opposition and fulfill the purpose that God entrusts to our hands.

If we accept the purpose of God for our lives, we can be sure that God's presence and power will be with us to fulfill it. Ephesians 3:7-12 states, *"Whereof I was made a minister, according to the gift of the grace of God given unto me by the effectual working of his power. Unto me, who am less than the least of all saints, is this grace given, that I should preach among the Gentiles the unsearchable riches of Christ; And to make all men see what is the fellowship of the mystery, which from the beginning of the world hath been hid in God, who created all things by Jesus Christ: To the intent that now unto the principalities and powers in heavenly places might be known by the church the manifold wisdom of God, According to the eternal purpose which he purposed in Christ Jesus our Lord: In whom we have boldness and access with confidence by the faith of him.* " The power to accomplish the mission is granted to those who engage in the purpose of God. The Lord Jesus told the disciples to wait in Jerusalem until they were endued with power from on high. God still releases the power of the Holy Spirit to everyone who serves Him.

He Directs Us To The Place Of Our Assignment

The Holy Spirit leads us to the place of our assignment. For example, He led Philip to the Ethiopian eunuch - Acts 8. He directed Peter to Cornelius - Acts 10. He led Paul to Macedonia - Acts 16. In Isaiah 41:1-3 God said, *"Keep silence before me, O islands; and let the people renew their strength: let them come near; then let them speak: let us come near together to judgment. Who raised up the righteous man from the east, called him to his foot, gave the nations before him, and made him rule over kings? he gave them as the dust to his sword, and as driven stubble to his bow. He pursued them, and passed safely; even by the way that he had not gone with his feet.* " Where He leads us, God's presence and power will demolish opposition, and His purpose will be fulfilled. For those in His purpose, Isaiah 41:10-15 says that He will help, strengthen, and empower them to surmount great obstacles. He will disarm and put their enemies to shame. Through the Holy Spirit, they will receive every assistance they require to fulfill the purpose of God.

He Gives Us Spiritual Gifts
Through the Holy Spirit, spiritual gifts are available to enable us to fulfill the purpose of God. These spiritual gifts enumerated in 1 Corinthians 12:7-10 are:

- the word of wisdom
- the word of knowledge
- faith
- gifts of healing
- the working of miracles
- prophecy
- discerning of spirits
- diverse kinds of tongues
- interpretation of tongues

Many believers assume that only apostles, prophets, evangelists, pastors, and teachers need these gifts. On the contrary, every believer needs them. In 1 Corinthians 14:1, the Apostle Paul encouraged us to desire spiritual gifts. We must ask God to equip us with the gifts of the Holy Spirit so that we can accomplish His will. Romans 12:6-8 says that God also gives us skills for ministering, teaching, exhorting, giving, leading, ruling, administering, and showing compassion. These gifts are crucial because they enhance our ability to fulfill the purpose of God.

He Fills Us With The Fruit Of The Holy Spirit
In addition to the power of the Holy Spirit and the gifts of the Holy Spirit, we are also empowered to fulfill the purpose of God as the Holy Spirit develops His fruit in us. By this, the Holy Spirit develops the character of God in us to make us effective in our assignments. Impatience, anger, bitterness, malice, indiscipline, selfishness, strife, and doubt will undermine the purpose of God. In us, the Holy Spirit develops the love, joy, peace, long-suffering, gentleness, goodness, faith, meekness, and temperance that we need to fulfill the purpose of God. This makes us

44

sensitive, empathetic, and reliable in serving others as God intended. Through the fruit of the Holy Spirit, carnality is mitigated. We become sensitive to the leading of the Holy Spirit. He keeps us in tune with the desire of God and positions us to bear fruit according to the will of God. Without the fruit of the Holy Spirit, we cannot fulfill the purpose of God. For this reason, God develops the fruit of the Holy Spirit in us when we submit to His purpose.

He Teaches Us
In John 14:26, Jesus Christ promised that the Holy Spirit will teach us all things. A believer committed to fulfilling the purpose of God by receiving the counsel of the Holy Spirit and doing what He teaches will be a mystery. The Holy Spirit imparts the wisdom of God in what He teaches. By obeying His instructions, we act in the wisdom of God. The wisdom of God is far superior to the wisdom of man, *"because the foolishness of God is wiser than men; and the weakness of God is stronger than men." -* 1 Corinthians 1:25. Jesus Christ promised that the Holy Spirit would teach us all things - John 14:26. If we follow His teachings, it will guarantee our success in fulfilling the purpose of God. So, there are no limitations if we consult Him.

He Guides Us
The believer who wants to fulfill the purpose of God need not be apprehensive. John 15:26 says that the Holy Spirit is the Spirit of truth. There can be no lie in His counsel or instruction. 1 John 2:27 says, *"But the anointing which you have received from Him abides in you, and you do not need that anyone teach you; but as the same anointing teaches you concerning all things, and is true, and is not a lie, and just as it has taught you, you will abide in*

Him." All revelations from the Holy Spirit must be true. His counsel must be reliable. For the Lord Jesus Christ to be glorified, it has to be reliable because by relying and acting on it, the testimony of the Lord Jesus Christ will be manifested. We cannot suffer shame in the purpose of God if we walk in the counsel of the Holy Spirit.

For example, many years ago, in a church service, the Holy Spirit said that we should clap on the tops of our own heads. After we did, He said none of us would suffer shame. The next day, a female member of the church attended to a client at a group home where she worked. Soon after, the client died. The management of the group home, suspecting foul play, quizzed her. She hurriedly went to the bathroom to pray, reminding God that He had said that none would suffer shame. After her prayer, the deceased client came back to life, and the investigation ceased. Overnight under the care of another staff member, the client died. This illustrates how Jesus is glorified when we obey the counsel of the Holy Spirit. Clapping on top of our heads seemed ridiculous, but it produced a miracle.

In another example, a pregnant woman was told that her fetus must be evacuated because it had no heartbeat. I was asked to pray. Before praying, the Lord told me to place my hand on my ear and that if I heard a heartbeat, the baby would live. When I placed my hand on my ear and heard a heartbeat, I prayed with the woman on the phone. On the day the fetus was to be removed, an ultrasound showed that it had a heartbeat. Obedience to the instruction, resulted in a miracle that glorified the Lord Jesus Christ.

In a third example, the Holy Spirit told me to put water in a bowl and say that it is no longer water but the blood of

Jesus and sprinkle the products that didn't sell. Within hours of doing it, the products were sold for cash. Not only that, we had new orders for more of the products than we sold. We have had uncountable and diverse testimonies by the sprinkling of the blood. The Holy Spirit always guides us into the truth. We have never suffered for following His counsel. This powerful grace is given to enable us to fulfill the purpose of God.

He Convicts And Corrects Us

One of the most important ministries of the Holy Spirit, to those who desire to fulfill the plan of God, is convicting and correcting them. Jesus Christ, in John 16:8 said, *"And when He comes, He will convict the world of sin, and of righteousness, and of judgment."* Correction acts as a guardrail that saves us from error and its painful consequences. It shields us from distractions, deception, and entrapment. Responding to the convictions of the Holy Spirit saves us time and gives us peace. It empowers us to maintain discipline by following the will of God. What we learn through the corrections we receive makes us more effective in fulfilling the purpose of God.

He Gives Us Revelation

In John 16:13, Jesus Christ promised that *"when He, the Spirit of truth has come, He will guide you into all truth, for He will not speak of His own authority, but whatever He hears He will speak; and He will tell you things to come."* By showing us things that are to come, the Holy Spirit gives us peace, confidence, boldness, and comfort. He reveals the truth to us to shield us from the lies of the devil, so that we can take necessary precautions and steps to fulfill the purpose of God. For many years, the Lord has always told us what to expect each year. They have come to pass exactly as He said. For example, while not specifically telling us of Covid-19, on December 31, 2019, at our annual Cross Over service, the Holy Spirit said, "Year 2020 will be turbulent, but be not afraid." When COVID came, we were not afraid, and the Lord protected us. We took necessary precautions but never stopped church services even once.

He Fills And Enables Us To Walk In The Spirit
With the Holy Spirit, God fills those who want to fulfill His purpose. He helps them to walk in the Spirit as the Holy Spirit helps and directs them. As a result, they cannot be stopped, outwitted, frustrated, or afflicted. They cannot be trapped or oppressed but always accomplish the purpose of God. The Holy Spirit guides and gives them breakthroughs in their mission. By following heavenly protocol, they have dominion where God leads them, and their authority is established. Being divine agents of blessing, the Holy Spirit supports them in bringing the manifestations of the kingdom of God to every place to bless those whom God sends to them. Joseph, Daniel, and the Apostles fulfilled the purpose of God because the Spirit of God was in them. This benefit is still available to those who engage in the purpose of God.

By the presence of the Holy Spirit in the believer, he or she has God's power to fulfill purpose. The power of the Holy Spirit is the power of God Himself. There is no power superior to this. The power of the Holy Spirit is greater than the power of the devil, principalities, powers, might, dominion, governments, and every other power in heaven, on earth, and under the earth. You are unbeatable when you know, understand, and use the power of the Holy Spirit in fulfilling the purpose of God. If you accept the assignment that God gave you, you will become an agent of God's blessing. God will provide you with the divine capabilities you need to do it.

Chapter Five

THE POWER OF GODLY PURPOSE

The purpose of God from the beginning is to establish His kingdom on earth. That purpose has not changed. Though Adam failed, Jesus Christ came to pave the way for the fulfillment of the purpose. His death, burial, and resurrection redeemed, saved, justified, and clothed man with the righteousness of God. Jesus Christ makes those who believe in Him through the preaching of the Gospel citizens of His kingdom. At the end of time, He will replace the existing heaven and earth with a new heaven and a new earth. The new Jerusalem will come down from heaven, and the tabernacle of God will be with men. Jesus Christ, as God, will be with them and rule among them as the King in His earthly kingdom forever!

Revelation 21:1-5 says, *"Now I saw a new heaven and a new earth, for the first heaven and the first earth had passed away. Also there was no more sea. ² Then I, John, saw the holy city, New Jerusalem, coming down out of heaven from God, prepared as a bride adorned for her husband. ³ And I heard a loud voice from heaven saying, "Behold, the tabernacle of God is with men, and He will dwell with them, and they shall be His people. God Himself will be with them and be their God. ⁴ And God will wipe away every tear from their eyes; there shall be no more death, nor sorrow, nor crying. There shall be no more pain, for the former things have passed away." ⁵ Then He who sat on the throne said, "Behold, I make all things new." And He said to me, "Write, for these words are true and faithful."* This scripture promises a new experience of life because sin, pain, sorrow, death, and tears will cease forever. Confusion and hopelessness will disappear, and the original plan of God will be fully operational. No one will remember any evil experiences. God will make all things new! Jesus Christ, the God-man, will be the ruler on earth. He will rule among the saints forever and ever in an atmosphere of righteousness where there is no sin at all. By this, His eternal purpose of establishing His kingdom on earth and among His people will finally be realized.

In furtherance of this objective, God enlists people in His service, and once enlisted, He supports them to fulfill the specific role He assigns to them. Though they may appear ordinary or routine, God supernaturally plans and orders all natural and spiritual activities to promote His purpose. He uses all created things, visible and invisible, including angels, plants, animals, insects, weather, and mankind, to fulfill His will. This phenomenon is what we describe as 'The power of purpose.' It is the power operating behind all divine accomplishments. It is the invisible divine acts targeted at accomplishing divine objectives. It is the power that the Almighty God engages behind the scenes to order things in favor of those who desire to fulfill His purpose. He structures, organizes, and puts into operation the things that are necessary for His servants to fulfill His purpose. These divine acts empower people to fulfill the purpose of God. It is God making all things work together for good to those who love Him and who are the called according to His purpose - Romans 8:28. This power works in, for, and with those who embrace the purpose for which God created them. It is available to everyone who commits to the purpose of God.

Examples of these divine acts and support are:
Divine Authority
When God calls anyone to fulfill His purpose, He gives the person the authority to do so, and that authority can

never be overruled or undermined by anyone or anything. It is a divine authority that is superior to and overrules all other authorities on the earth!

For example, when God gave Moses the authority to lead the Jews out of Egypt, Pharaoh, despite his power, could not stop him. Exodus 7:1 says, *"And the LORD said unto Moses, see, I have made thee a god to Pharaoh: and Aaron thy brother shall be thy prophet."* That authority empowered Moses to accomplish the assignment. By his word, he brought plagues on rivers, animals, plants, and homes in Egypt. By his word, plagues came, and by his word, they ceased. The word of Moses ruled Egypt, and Pharaoh became irrelevant.

After they came out of Egypt, Miriam, his elder sister, and Aaron, his elder brother, spoke against Moses' authority, and God disciplined them - Numbers 12:1-15. When Korah, Kohath, Dathan, Abiram, and On rebelled against Moses, God destroyed them, their supporters, and their families - Numbers 16.

God appointed and gave Aaron authority to serve as priest. He silenced opposition and confirmed Aaron's authority when, among the rods of the tribes, Aaron's rod budded and bore ripe almonds overnight - Numbers 17:1-10.

After Moses died, God appointed Joshua and gave him authority to lead Israel - Joshua 1:1-5. In verse 5 God said, *"No man shall be able to stand before you all the days of your life; as I was with Moses, so I will be with you. I will not leave you nor forsake you."* The elders of Israel recognized and respected his authority, saying, *"All that you command us we will do, and wherever you send us we will go. Just as we heeded Moses in all things, so we will heed you. Only the LORD your God be with you, as*

He was with Moses. Whoever rebels against your command and does not heed your words, in all that you command him, shall be put to death. Only be strong and of good courage." Joshua 1:16-18. Except for a defeat at Ai due to Achan's disobedience, in Joshua chapter 7, he conquered Canaan by the authority that God gave him.

God gave Jeremiah authority over nations and kingdoms, to root out, and to pull down, and to destroy, and to throw down, to build and to plant - Jeremiah 1:4-10. When his authority was contested, God confirmed it by fulfilling the words which Jeremiah spoke against Hananiah, the false prophet who opposed him - Jeremiah 28:15-17.

In Matthew 10:5-8, 28:18-20, Luke 10:19, Mark 16:15-18, and John 20:21, Jesus Christ gave His disciples authority to preach the gospel of the kingdom. He commanded them to use their authority to heal the sick, cast out devils, cleanse the leper, raise the dead, and proclaim the gospel. God worked with them and confirmed their words with signs and wonders - Mark 16:20 and Luke 10:17.

Believers have authority to discipline, bind, and eliminate contrary forces, powers, wisdom, schemes, protocol, programs, logistics, and agents of Satan that challenge, resist, obstruct, restrict, or attempt to frustrate divine agenda. Peter demonstrated this authority when he rebuked Ananias and Sapphira in Acts 5, and Simon the sorcerer in Acts 8. Apostle Paul did the same with Elymas the sorcerer in Acts 13.

Perhaps the most noticeable demonstration of authority was through Elijah the prophet. He commanded that it should not rain for three and half years in Israel, and it did not. After three and a half years, he commanded it to rain again - 1 Kings 17. He destroyed the prophets of Baal - 1

Kings 18 and two contingents of fifty soldiers sent by Ahaziah, king of Samaria, to arrest him - 2 Kings 1.

Divine authority is available to us in God's purpose. We have authority to trample on the powers of darkness, and nothing shall by any means harm us - Luke 10:19. God always causes us to triumph in every place in Christ to affirm the authority that He gave us to fulfill His purpose - 2 Corinthians 2:14-16. Those who are in the purpose of God have authority to fulfill the desire of God. Apostles, prophets, evangelists, pastors, teachers, and elders of the church have such authority. Apostle Paul, in 2 Corinthians 10:8 said, *"For though I should boast somewhat more of our authority, which the Lord hath given us for edification, and not for your destruction, I should not be ashamed."* He also said, *"Therefore I write these things being absent, lest being present I should use sharpness, according to the authority which the Lord has given me for edification and not for destruction."* - 2 Corinthians 13:10. Elders use their authority to heal, teach, and administer the church. The Lord works with them to build the church by confirming their words with signs following. Believers have authority to:
- Preach the gospel - Matthew 10:7; 28:16-20.
- Heal the sick - Matthew 10:8.
- Cast out devils - Mark 16:16-20; Matthew 10:8.
- Cleanse lepers - Matthew 10:8.
- Raise the dead - Matthew 10:8.
- Accomplish divine assignments.
- Use the name of Jesus Christ - Mark 16:16-20; John 14:14.

Everyone in the purpose of God has the authority of God to act. It is the authority of God Himself, and there is no authority superior to it. They have the right to use their God-given authority against an institution, force, or person attempting to hinder, delay, deny, or undermine them. I have had the privilege of demonstrating this authority, and the Lord has always backed it up to humble the wicked. This privilege is available to you if you are in the purpose of God. Nothing can hinder your success because divine authority cannot be overruled.

Divine Support

"If it had not been the LORD who was on our side," Let Israel now say— [2] "If it had not been the LORD who was on our side, When men rose up against us, [3] Then they would have swallowed us alive, When their wrath was kindled against us; Psalms 124:1-3. Divine support is promised to those who engage in the purpose of God. Jesus Christ said, *"I will not leave you nor forsake you."* God's unwavering support is shown in Psalm 2:6 by these words: *"Yet have I set my King upon my holy hill of Zion."* His resolute support is guaranteed to anyone who desires to fulfill His purpose. In Isaiah 41:17, God said, *"I the LORD will hear them. I, the God of Israel will not forsake them."* His dealings with Abraham illustrate this. In Genesis 12:14-20, God stopped Pharaoh from taking Sarah, Abraham's wife. He also stopped Abimelech from doing the same thing in Genesis 20. Without the support of God, either Pharaoh or Abimelech, who were very powerful kings against whom Abraham had no defense, could have taken Sarah. The purpose of raising an heir through her would have failed, but that satanic plot was thwarted. After Lot left him, God affirmed His promise to Abraham - Genesis 13:14-17, and He is still fulfilling the promises to Jews and Gentiles even now - Galatians 3:29.

God's support includes encouraging people to fulfill His purpose. For example, in Haggai 2:4-5, He encouraged Zerubbabel, saying, *"'Yet now be strong, Zerubbabel,' says the LORD; 'and be strong, Joshua, son of*

Jehozadak, the high priest; and be strong, all you people of the land,' says the LORD, 'and work; for I am with you,' says the LORD of hosts. 'According to the word that I covenanted with you when you came out of Egypt, so My Spirit remains among you; do not fear!'" He encouraged Gideon, saying, *"The Lord is with thee, thou mighty man of valour." Judges 6:12.* He also said, *"Go in this thy might, and thou shalt save Israel from the hand of the Midianites: have not I sent thee?" Judges 6:14.* Declaring His support for Joshua, He said, *"There shall not any man be able to stand before thee all the days of thy life: as I was with Moses, so I will be with thee: I will not fail thee, nor forsake thee. Be strong and of a good courage: for unto this people shalt thou divide for an inheritance the land, which I sware unto their fathers to give them. Only be thou strong and very courageous, that thou mayest observe to do according to all the law, which Moses my servant commanded thee: turn not from it to the right hand or to the left, that thou mayest prosper whithersoever thou goest. This book of the law shall not depart out of thy mouth; but thou shalt meditate therein day and night, that thou mayest observe to do according to all that is written therein: for then thou shalt make thy way prosperous, and then thou shalt have good success. Have not I commanded thee? Be strong and of a good courage; be not afraid, neither be thou dismayed: for the LORD thy God is with thee whithersoever thou goest." Joshua 1:5-10.* In Joshua 3:7, He also assured Joshua, saying, *"This day will I begin to magnify thee in the sight of all Israel, that they may know that, as I was with Moses, so I will be with thee."* God's words motivated Joshua and gave him the confidence to fulfill the purpose of God. God will give you the same support if you commit to His purpose.

There are numerous examples of God's support for those He chose to fulfill His purpose. God anointed Cyrus, humbled great kings before him, facilitated his exploits, granted him breakthroughs everywhere, and helped him conquer Babylon. Isaiah 45:1-6 says, *"Thus saith the LORD to his anointed, to Cyrus, whose right hand I have holden, to subdue nations before him; and I will loose the loins of kings, to open before him the two leaved gates; and the gates shall not be shut; I will go before thee, and make the crooked places straight: I will break in pieces the gates of brass, and cut in sunder the bars of iron: And I will give thee the treasures of darkness, and hidden riches of secret places, that thou mayest know that I, the LORD, which call thee by thy name, am the God of Israel. For Jacob my servant's sake, and Israel mine elect, I have even called thee by thy name: I have surnamed thee, though thou hast not known me. I am the LORD, and there is none else, there is no God beside me: I girded thee, though thou hast not known me: That they may know from the rising of the sun, and from the west, that there is none beside me. I am the LORD, and there is none else."* God gave him riches to prosecute the wars and strength to overcome. God still does these things to advance His purpose through His chosen vessels.

God frustrated all the attempts of religious leaders to stop the apostles from preaching the gospel - Acts 4. He worked with them and confirmed their words with signs and wonders - Mark 16:20. Persecution scattered them and enabled them to preach the gospel beyond Jerusalem. He still works with us to fulfill His purpose, and we can fulfill the purpose of God anywhere He sends us. With His support, we cannot fail because God did not call us to struggle, fail, or suffer defeat in His purpose. We have

His promise that He would neither leave us nor forsake us. We should be confident in the support of Almighty God as we pursue our calling.

The Bible says, *"When they went from one nation to another, from one kingdom to another people; He suffered no man to do them wrong: yea, he reproved kings for their sakes; Saying, touch not mine anointed, and do my prophets no harm." Psalm 105:13-15.* God protects us from all enemies so that we can fulfill His purpose. He gave Israel the land of Canaan by His mighty strength. Psalm 44:1-3 says, *"We have heard with our ears, O God, our fathers have told us, what work thou didst in their days, in the times of old. How thou didst drive out the heathen with thy hand, and plantedst them; how thou didst afflict the people, and cast them out. For they got not the land in possession by their own sword, neither did their own arm save them: but thy right hand, and thine arm, and the light of thy countenance, because thou hadst a favour unto them."* God's support never faltered. Though fewer, the Jews dispossessed nations that were greater than they.

Through divine support, God places in our hands what He promises or reserves for us. For example, in the year 2015, through my error, we almost lost a property that God wanted us to acquire. In desperation, I prayed, and the Lord said to me, *"What I reserved for you in Christ, I will put in your hand."* Indeed, He put the property in our hands. His word erased fear, anxiety, and confusion. He perfectly ordered things in our favor, and we acquired the property.

God also supports us by warning our enemies not to harm us. An example was when Jacob left Laban to go back to Canaan. Genesis 31:20-24 says, *"And Jacob stole away unawares to Laban the Syrian, in that he told him not that he fled. So he fled with all that he had; and he rose up, and passed over the river, and set his face toward the mount Gilead. And it was told Laban on the third day that Jacob was fled. And he took his brethren with him, and pursued after him seven days' journey; and they overtook him in the mount Gilead. And God came to Laban the Syrian in a dream by night, and said unto him, Take heed that thou speak not to Jacob either good or bad."* Laban was forced to make peace with Jacob because of the warning he received from God. In Genesis 34, the sons of Jacob killed the men of Shalem. They also killed Shechem, his son Hamor, who had defiled their sister Dinah, and plundered the city. Fearing retribution, Jacob panicked. God instructed him to go back to Bethel, He put His terror on the cities along the way, and they could not attack Jacob and his family.

God's support for Isaac made him prosper in the time of famine. Genesis 26:12-14 says, *"Then Isaac sowed in that land, and received in the same year an hundredfold: and the LORD blessed him. And the man waxed great, and went forward, and grew until he became very great: For he had possession of flocks, and possession of herds, and great store of servants: and the Philistines envied him."* In the time of economic collapse, God gave Isaac an enviable blessing. When the Philistines seized several wells of water from him, God encouraged him. *"And the LORD appeared unto him the same night, and said, I am the God of Abraham thy father: fear not, for I am with thee, and will bless thee, and multiply thy seed for my servant Abraham's sake." Genesis 26:24.* There is no greater assurance of divine support than for God to say, '*fear not, I am with you.*' That is what He said in Isaiah 41:10, 13, and 14. Jesus Christ also said so in John 8:20

and 14:1. No earthly support is greater than this. When you are in the purpose of God, you have nothing to fear. His divine support will defend you in times of hostility.

God is certainly with those who are in His purpose. God's support for Isaac caused the Philistines, led by their king, his friend, and military commander, to enter into a peace treaty with him. Genesis 26:26-29 says, *"Then Abimelech went to him from Gerar, and Ahuzzath one of his friends, and Phichol the chief captain of his army. And Isaac said unto them, Wherefore come ye to me, seeing ye hate me, and have sent me away from you? And they said, We saw certainly that the LORD was with thee: and we said, Let there be now an oath betwixt us, even betwixt us and thee, and let us make a covenant with thee; That thou wilt do us no hurt, as we have not touched thee, and as we have done unto thee nothing but good, and have sent thee away in peace: thou art now the blessed of the LORD."* The delegation knew that Isaac had God's support because the king said, *"We saw certainly that the LORD was with thee."*

God's support gave Shadrach, Meshach, and Abednego victory in the fiery furnace - Daniel 3:14-30. His support gave Daniel victory in the lion's den - Daniel 6. No matter the challenge we face in the purpose of God, we will have victory because God never leaves or forsakes us. Isaiah 54:10 gives assurance of divine support, saying, *"For the mountains shall depart and the hills be removed, but My kindness shall not depart from you, nor shall My covenant of peace be removed," Says the LORD, who has mercy on you."* God's kindness shall not depart from you, neither shall His covenant of peace be removed. You will always enjoy God's support when you embrace His purpose. You can be confident that He will never abandon you if you choose to fulfill His purpose.

God supported Moses when He opened the sea and destroyed Pharaoh and his army - Exodus 14. He did not allow Balak and Balaam to curse the Israelites - Numbers 22 to 24. He frustrated the plot of Haman to destroy the Jews in Medo-Persia - Esther 3 to 9. He moved Cyrus to free the Jews to build the temple in Jerusalem - Ezra 1.

Psalms 118:6 says, *"The LORD is on my side; I will not fear. What can man do to me?"* You have God's support. This should eliminate fear and establish peace in your heart. Be confident in pursuing and accomplishing divine objectives. You cannot fail. Your partner in the pursuit of godly purpose is the Almighty God. In Him, you have all that you need to succeed. God's support is your power.

Divine Presence
Jeremiah 20:11 says, *"But the LORD is with me as a mighty, awesome One. Therefore my persecutors will stumble, and will not prevail. They will be greatly ashamed, for they will not prosper. Their everlasting confusion will never be forgotten."* God's presence is always with those who commit to His purpose. When God sends people on an assignment, He goes with them. The Lord Jesus Christ said, *"He that sent me is with me: the Father hath not left me alone."* John 8:29. Exodus 23:20 says, *"Behold, I send an angel before you to keep you in the way and to bring you into the place which I have prepared."* God keeps those who engage in His purpose. They cannot fail. They accomplish divine purpose. In Matthew 28:19-20, Jesus said, *"Go therefore and make disciples of all the nations, baptizing them in the name of the Father and of the Son and of the Holy Spirit, "teaching them to observe all things that I have commanded you; and lo, I am with you always, even to the end of the age." Amen.*

God is always with us to empower and uphold us in His purpose. He told Jacob, *"Behold, I am with you and will keep you wherever you go, and will bring you back to this land; for I will not leave you until I have done what I have spoken to you." Genesis 28:15.* God is fully invested in His purpose and ensures that nothing disturbs it. He does whatever is needed to realize His purpose. He terrorizes the enemy, removes obstacles, and guides us in His purpose. God's presence with us guarantees that we will fulfill His purpose. The presence of God destroys the weapons and devices of the enemies to give us success in all divine engagements. In Matthew 8:23-27; Jesus Christ rebuked the winds and the sea, and it was calm. In Matthew 14:22-33, Jesus Christ walked on the stormy sea to strengthen His disciples. He still walks on the stormy seas, and His presence still calms the storm.

The presence of God moves the hearts of men to support and help us fulfill the purpose of God. David said to Solomon, *"Be strong and of good courage, and do it: fear not, nor be dismayed: for the LORD God, even my God, will be with thee; he will not fail thee, nor forsake thee, until thou hast finished all the work for the service of the house of the LORD. And, behold, the courses of the priests and the Levites, even they shall be with thee for all the service of the house of God: and there shall be with thee for all manner of workmanship every willing skilful man, for any manner of service: also the princes and all the people will be wholly at thy commandment."1 Chronicles 28:20-21.* David said that once Solomon decides to devote himself to building the temple, God will be with him and will not fail nor forsake him until the work is finished. He said that God will provide anointed and skilled people who will work with him to fulfill the assignment.

Asa, the king of Judah, instituted reform, caused the people to dedicate themselves to God, and restored the temple service. The presence of God with him inspired the people to gather to him abundantly - 2 Chronicles 15:9.

Divine presence attracts favor. It provides order and peace. It subdues the enemies under our authority as we advance the purpose of God. It gives breakthroughs so that we are not hindered in God's purpose. Job 9:4 says, *"He is wise in heart, and mighty in strength: who hath hardened himself against him, and hath prospered?"* Opposition is frustrated. Proverbs 21:30 says, *"There is no wisdom nor understanding nor counsel against the LORD."* Divine presence creates a conducive atmosphere for fulfilling the purpose of God. Mark 16:20 says, *"And they went forth, and preached every where, the Lord working with them, and confirming the word with signs following. Amen."* Through divine presence, the purpose will be publicly authenticated, and all people will see it.

Ezra 2:4-6:22 shows that no one can frustrate the purpose of God. The presence of God produces rest - Exodus 33:14. It fills enemies with fear. They cannot overcome us. We will fulfill the purpose in peace. God's presence banishes fear and produces confidence and boldness. Moses had no fear because he knew that God was with him and he boldly confronted Pharaoh. The Apostles were not afraid when the Sanhedrin and elders questioned them. They spoke boldly - Acts 4:13. Like Moses and the Apostles, we have divine authority and power to fulfill the purpose of God. We must be bold.

With the presence of the Lord, we have unrestricted access to His unlimited wisdom. This puts us ahead of the enemy and helps us to accomplish the purpose of God. The Sanhedrin were disarmed by the wisdom of the

Apostles - Acts 4:6-13. They could not stop them from fulfilling the purpose of God. In all circumstances, the presence of God vindicates us. He saves us from the lash of the tongue and reproach. *"Thou shalt be hid from the scourge of the tongue: neither shalt thou be afraid of destruction when it cometh. At destruction and famine thou shalt laugh: neither shalt thou be afraid of the beasts of the earth. For thou shalt be in league with the stones of the field: and the beasts of the field shall be at peace with thee." Job 5:21-23.* The presence of God endues us with uniqueness and grace to fulfill His purpose. When people around us plot our failure, God humbles them by giving us outstanding success. The story of Joseph in Genesis 39:1-6, 20-23; 40:1-22; 41:25-46 and Daniel in Daniel chapters 2 and 6 are examples.

Angelic Assistance

Angelic assistance is available to those God uses for His purpose. For example, in Luke 1, the Angel Gabriel brought word to Zechariah about the birth of John and to Mary about the birth of Jesus Christ. In Matthew 1:18-24, an angel counseled Joseph in a dream not to reject Mary, his wife. Angels announced the birth of Jesus Christ to the shepherds keeping their flock at night - Luke 2:8-18. In Matthew 2:13-14, an angel told Joseph to take the young child and his mother (Jesus Christ and Mary) to Egypt to escape from Herod's murderous plot. After the death of Herod, in Matthew 2:19-23, an angel instructed Joseph to return to Israel. Through these angelic helps, Joseph was able to fulfill the plan of God. Jacob received favor from Esau, his brother, after angels met him on his return journey from Syria - Genesis 32:1-33:17. Joshua received angelic assistance at Jericho - Joshua 5:13-15. Angels ministered to Jesus Christ at the temptation - Matthew

4:11; Mark 1:13. He was also strengthened by angels in the Garden of Gethsemane - Luke 22:43.

An angel released the Apostles from prison - Acts 5:17-20. An angel delivered Peter from prison and from death - Acts 12:1-11. An angel instructed Cornelius in Acts 10 to send for Apostle Peter, who preached to his household. Abraham experienced angelic visitations - Genesis 18. Angel Gabriel ministered to Daniel in Daniel 10. Apostle Paul advised that we should not forget to *"entertain strangers: for thereby some have entertained angels unawares." - Hebrews 13:2.* Angels appearing as human beings are all around us, and they help us to fulfill the purpose of God. God promised angelic protection to those who engage in His will - Psalm 91:1-11.

Divine Provision
God provides what is needed, when it is needed, in the measure that is needed, to those who are in His purpose. He commanded the Israelites to give tithes and offerings to the Levites as a reward for their service to the Lord - Number 18:24; 31:28-30; and 35:1-8. Twice, Jesus Christ fed thousands in the wilderness where there was no place to buy food - Matthew 14:15-21; 15:32-38; 16:6-12. When He sent out the disciples to preach, He told them not to carry money or a change of clothes. He provided for them. They lacked nothing. Luke 22:35 says, ***"When I sent you without money bag, knapsack, and sandals, did you lack anything?" So they said, "Nothing."***

For 40 years, He provided and cared for the Israelites in the wilderness - Deuteronomy 8:4 says, ***"Your garments did not wear out on you, nor did your foot swell these forty years."*** Psalm 105:40-41 says, ***"The people asked, and He brought quail, and satisfied them with the bread of heaven. He opened the rock, and water gushed out; it*** *ran in the dry places like a river."* He gave them manna, water, and meat. He fed Elijah in the wilderness with bread and meat twice daily, using ravens - 1 Kings 17:1-6. He sent him to the widow in Zarephath of Sidon while famine was still raging in the land, and the barrel of flour and cruise of oil never ran out - 1 Kings 17:9-16. Isaiah 41:18 says, *"I will open rivers in desolate heights, and fountains in the midst of the valleys; I will make the wilderness a pool of water, and the dry land springs of water.* There is no lack for those in the purpose of God.

When we are in the purpose of God, provision should be our least concern. Jesus Christ said, *"Seek first the kingdom of God and His righteousness and all these things shall be added to you." - Matthew 6:33.* Psalm 34:10 says, *"The young lions lack and suffer hunger; but those who seek the LORD shall not lack any good thing."* Psalm 37:25 confirmed it saying, *"I have been young, and now am old; yet I have not seen the righteous forsaken, nor his descendants begging bread."* The purpose of God is not fulfilled at our own expense - *Who ever goes to war at his own expense? -1 Corinthians 9:7.* God always provides the resources to accomplish His purpose because the gold and the silver are His, and He owns the sheep on a thousand hills - Psalm 50:10. Divine support and provision will never fail you when you choose to fulfill the purpose of God.

Divine Protection And Preservation
Divine protection is assured to those who are in the purpose of God. He does this in many ways.

God makes you invincible: To Jeremiah, God said, *"For behold, I have made you this day a fortified city and an iron pillar, and bronze walls against the whole land; Against the kings of Judah, against its princes, against* *its priests, and against the people of the land. They will fight against you, but they shall not prevail against you. For I am with you," says the LORD, "to deliver you." Jeremiah 1:18-19.* Again, in Jeremiah 15:20-21 He said, *"And I will make you to this people a fortified bronze wall; And they will fight against you, but they shall not prevail against you; For I am with you to save you and deliver you," says the LORD. "I will deliver you from the hand of the wicked, and I will redeem you from the grip of the terrible." Jeremiah 15:20-21.*

He preserves you from death: God preserves us from death so that we can fulfill His purpose. In Exodus 1 and 2 Pharaoh decreed that all the male children of the Jews should be killed at birth. After the midwives sabotaged the decree, he told the people to cast the male children into the river, but God preserved Moses, and he was raised in the palace of Pharaoh. God used Moses to deliver Israel from four hundred and thirty years of captivity. To fulfill His purpose in Jesus Christ, God saved Him from Herod, who wanted to kill Him. He instructed Joseph to take the young child to Egypt, thereby preserving His life. By His death, burial, and resurrection, Jesus Christ redeemed us. Because of His purpose, God saved Peter from Herod's plot to kill him. Using an angel, He brought Peter out of prison.

He exposes conspiracies: On his visit to Jerusalem, Paul was falsely accused of teaching against the law and the temple. He was arrested by religious zealots and arraigned by the mob. Though the Sanhedrin was not persuaded by his defense, it divided the Pharisees against the Sadducee. The commander fearing that the people would harm him, took Paul from their midst and held him in the barracks. Some of the Jews took an oath not to eat or drink until they have killed him. They went to the priest and said,

66

"Now you, therefore, together with the council, suggest to the commander that he be brought down to you tomorrow, as though you were going to make further inquiries concerning him; but we are ready to kill him before he comes near." Acts 23:15. Paul's nephew heard their plot and related it to him. Paul then asked that his nephew be taken to the commander to tell him of the plot. On hearing the plot, the commander sent Paul that night with a military escort to the governor in Caesarea, thereby frustrating the conspiracy.

He shields us from attacks: *"When they went from one nation to another, from one kingdom to another people, God permitted no one to do them wrong. He rebuked kings for their sakes and forbade them from touching or harming them Psalm 105:13-14.* While ministering in Corinth, the Lord assured Paul in Acts 18:9-10 *"Do not be afraid, but speak, and do not keep silent; "for I am with you, and no one will attack you to hurt you; for I have many people in this city."* God said, *"I am with you, and no one will attack you to hurt you."* In the hazardous journey to Rome, while others panicked, Paul had peace, saying, *"For there stood by me this night an angel of the God to whom I belong and whom I serve, saying, 'Do not be afraid, Paul; you must be brought before Caesar; and indeed God has granted you all those who sail with you.'" Acts 27:23-24.* As He promised, God protected Paul and his companions.

He protects us from the weapons of the enemy: Isaiah 54:17 says, *"No weapon formed against you shall prosper, and every tongue which rises against you in judgment you shall condemn. This is the heritage of the servants of the LORD, and their righteousness is from Me," Says the LORD.* In Daniel 3, Meshach, Shadrach, and Abednego were thrown into the fiery furnace, which was heated seven times more than normal by Nebuchadnezzar, but God delivered them.

He makes the enemy's plot backfire: In Daniel 6, God protected Daniel from the conspiracy of his enemies and stopped the lions from attacking him. Those who plotted against him were destroyed in the lions' den with their families. Haman's plot against the Jews backfired; he and his sons were hanged on the gallows. By defending themselves against their enemies, the Jews were preserved.

He raises us above the enemy: Psalm 27:5-6 says, *"For in the time of trouble, He shall hide me in His pavilion; In the secret place of His tabernacle He shall hide me; He shall set me high upon a rock. And now my head shall be lifted up above my enemies round about me; Therefore I will offer sacrifices of joy in His tabernacle; I will sing, yes, I will sing praises to the Lord."* God preserved Joseph from the hatred of his brothers - Genesis 37. Though they wanted his vision to fail, God made him a leader and subdued his enemies.

He rebukes our opponents: God rebuked Laban for the sake of Jacob - Genesis 31. He softened the heart of Esau towards him when he was returning from Syria - Genesis 33. He saved him from the people of Shechem - Genesis 35. He rebuked Pharaoh - Genesis 12 and Abimelech - Genesis 20, for taking Abraham's wife.

He paralyzes the enemy with fear: God preserved Jacob on the way to Bethel. Genesis 35:5 said, *"And they journeyed; and the terror of God was upon the cities that were round about them, and they did not pursue after the sons of Jacob."* Just as the terror of God was on all the nations when Moses led the people of Israel to Canaan, so His terror will be on those who may want to oppose His purpose for our lives.

He frustrates the enemy: By the instruction of the Lord, Samuel anointed David king over Israel and the grace of God was manifested on him from then on. He killed Goliath and won all the battles he fought for Israel. Saul envied him and sought to kill him. God frustrated all the attempts of Saul to kill David. Saul eventually lost his life in a battle with the Philistines. This is proof of God's protection for those who commit to fulfilling His purpose. You are assured of divine protection in God's purpose. God will preserve you so that you can accomplish the task that He assigned to you. Engaging in the purpose of God, in itself, shields us from the evil of this world.

He Preserves Us
In Isaiah 51:7-8 God said, *"Listen to Me, you who know righteousness, you people in whose heart is my law: Do not fear the reproach of men, nor be afraid of their insults. For the moth will eat them up like a garment, and the worm will eat them like wool; but my righteousness will be forever, and my salvation from generation to generation."* Psalm 121 says that God, who watches over us, neither slumbers nor sleeps. He is our keeper and the shade upon our right hand. He protects and preserves us from all evil. Psalm 91:9-14 assures, *"Because thou hast made the LORD, which is my refuge, even the most High, thy habitation; there shall no evil befall thee, neither shall any plague come nigh thy dwelling. For he shall give his angels charge over thee, to keep thee in all thy ways. They shall bear thee up in their hands, lest thou dash thy foot against a stone. Thou shalt tread upon the lion and adder: the young lion and the dragon shalt thou trample under feet. Because he hath set his love upon me, therefore will I deliver him: I will set him on high, because he hath known my name."* Psalm 91:3-7 says, *"Surely, he will*

deliver us from the snare of the fowler, and from the noisome pestilence. He will cover us with his feathers, and under his wings shalt we trust: his truth shall be our shield and buckler. We shalt not be afraid for the terror by night; nor for the arrow that flies by day; nor for the pestilence that walks in darkness; nor for the destruction that wastes at noonday. A thousand shall fall at our side, and ten thousand at our right hand; but it shall not come nigh us." Isaiah 60:18 says, *"Violence shall no more be heard in our land, wasting nor destruction within our borders; but we shalt call our walls Salvation, and our gates Praise."* When we give ourselves to serve the purpose of God, we will enjoy all-around protection.

Isaiah 43:1-4 says, *"But now, thus says the LORD, who created you, O Jacob, And He who formed you, O Israel: "Fear not, for I have redeemed you; I have called you by your name; You are Mine. When you pass through the waters, I will be with you; And through the rivers, they shall not overflow you. When you walk through the fire, you shall not be burned, Nor shall the flame scorch you. For I am the LORD your God, The Holy One of Israel, your Savior; I gave Egypt for your ransom, Ethiopia and Seba in your place. Since you were precious in My sight, You have been honored, And I have loved you; Therefore I will give men for you, And people for your life."* Without question, we have absolute protection if we devote ourselves to fulfilling the purpose of God. God will preserve us from all evil. If we stand for Him, He will stand for us and with us. There is no loss in the pursuit of the purpose of God.

1 Samuel 2:9-10 says, *"He will keep the feet of his saints, and the wicked shall be silent in darkness; for by strength shall no man prevail. The adversaries of the LORD shall be broken to pieces; out of heaven shall he*

thunder upon them: the LORD shall judge the ends of the earth; and he shall give strength unto his king, and exalt the horn of his anointed.' The protection of God that we enjoy in the pursuit of His purpose frustrates enemies. He breaks out against opposition and brings the counsel of the enemies to nothing. He makes their efforts fruitless - Isaiah 44:24-25; Psalm 33:10. Isaiah 29:7-8. God always stands by those who stand for His purpose.

Divine Guidance

God partners with us and guides us to fulfill His purpose. In Haggai 1:13-14 the Scripture says, *"Then Haggai, the Lord's messenger, spoke the Lord's message to the people, saying, "I am with you, says the LORD." So the LORD stirred up the spirit of Zerubbabel the son of Shealtiel, governor of Judah, and the spirit of Joshua the son of Jehozadak, the high priest, and the spirit of all the remnant of the people; and they came and worked on the house of the LORD of hosts, their God,"* God's omnipotence is available to those who desire to accomplish His purpose. They cannot fail. We should not entertain any fear of failure when we commit to the purpose of God. Philippians 2:13 assures, *"for it is God who works in you both to will and to do for His good pleasure."* God works in us to accomplish His purpose. Hebrews 13:20-21 says, *"Now may the God of peace who brought up our Lord Jesus from the dead, that great Shepherd of the sheep, through the blood of the everlasting covenant, make you complete in every good work to do His will, working in you what is well pleasing in His sight, through Jesus Christ, to whom be glory forever and ever." Amen.* He will work in us what is pleasing to Him.

While secular training may be necessary, it is not a substitute for the divine grace and support required for

71

progress, impact, and success in the purpose of God. God, who created us for His purpose, equipped us for it. We should not deny or minimize the amazing abilities that God has embedded in us. No secular education or training can supersede divine grace. God, who is greater than any secular source, is the source of all that we need to fulfill His purpose. 2 Corinthians 3:5-6 says, *"Not that we are sufficient of ourselves to think of anything as being from ourselves, but our sufficiency is from God, who also made us sufficient as ministers of the new covenant, not of the letter but of the Spirit; for the letter kills, but the Spirit gives life."*

God ensures the success of our assignment by showing us what to do and how to do it. Even before he began his assignment, God assured Moses that he would succeed because Exodus 3:10-12 says, *"Come now, therefore, and I will send you to Pharaoh that you may bring My people, the children of Israel, out of Egypt."* [11] *But Moses said to God, "Who am I that I should go to Pharaoh, and that I should bring the children of Israel out of Egypt?"* [12] *So He said, "I will certainly be with you. And this shall be a sign to you that I have sent you: When you have brought the people out of Egypt, you shall serve God on this mountain."* Before Moses commenced the assignment, God assured him that he would successfully bring the people out of Egypt and that they would worship Him on the mountain. To ensure his success, God guided Moses at every point. By obeying the instructions of God, Moses successfully accomplished the divine plan. At the Red Sea, for example, when it appeared that the army of Pharaoh would destroy them, by lifting up the rod as God instructed, Moses divided the sea, and the people crossed over to the other side. By lifting up the rod again as God instructed, Moses brought the sea upon the army of Pharaoh, and they were all destroyed. The success of our assignment is proof that the assignment is from God because He said to Moses, *"This shall be a sign to you that I have sent you."* If God has sent you, you cannot fail.

By following God's instructions, the Jordan River parted, and the wall of Jericho fell before Joshua. God gives us directives in the course of our assignment so that we can succeed in it. A person who is sensitive to the leading of the Holy Spirit and who faithfully obeys the instructions he receives cannot fail. Every assignment God gives us must succeed. He has a vested interest in our success. He guides our efforts to ensure our success. Those who obey His instructions succeed, and those who disobey fail. As we humbly follow the guidance of the Holy Spirit, power and wisdom are made available to fulfill the purpose of God. Being led by God is the guarantee of success.

God will never ask us to do what will fail. In fact, He created us for what He wants us to do. Manufacturers design their products to succeed. Everything a product requires to perform is built into it. Similarly, God created us to succeed in what He wants us to do. He designed us for the assignment that He has for us. We are well-suited for the assignment. The assignment God gives to us is to accomplish His own original purpose. If He assigns us to the wrong thing, we will fail, and if we fail, He will not accomplish His purpose. God ensures that we succeed in what He wants us to do. Therefore, success is proof that our assignment is from God. He called Abraham, and through his obedience to the counsel of God, he fulfilled his ministry. In his lineage, God raised the Lord Jesus Christ, our Savior, who is the seed of Abraham, through whom God is still blessing all the families of the earth, as He promised to do in Genesis 12:3.

God called Joseph. By skillfully managing the economy of Egypt through the inspiration and guidance of the Holy Spirit during the famine, Joseph fed the children of Israel and fulfilled his ministry. God called Bezalel, the son of Uri, to build the tabernacle in the wilderness. He equipped him with the Holy Spirit, and by His instructions, he built the tabernacle and accomplished his assignment. God called Joshua, and by following God's instructions, he brought the children of Israel into Canaan and allotted the land to them. Similarly, God called Gideon, Samson, Deborah, Samuel, Saul, David, Nehemiah, Ezra, Esther, Mordecai, Isaiah, Cyrus, Jeremiah, Ezekiel, Daniel, Obadiah, and others. He worked with them to fulfill His purpose in every generation. God is still doing the same.

Now therefore, go, and I will be with your mouth and teach you what you shall say. Exodus 4:12. God taught Moses what to say and what to do – *"Now you shall speak to him and put words in his mouth. And I will be with your mouth and with his mouth, and I will teach you what you shall do."* By following the teachings of God, Moses succeeded. Isaiah 28:26 says, *"For his God doth instruct him to discretion, and doth teach him."* When God is teaching you what to say and what to do, you cannot fail. Not only will you not fail, you will be a mystery because you will be speaking and doing things by the wisdom of God. For us to succeed, we must cherish and embrace the teachings of God. Isaiah 54:13 says, *"All your children shall be taught by the Lord, and great shall be the peace of your children."* The reason God teaches us is to ensure that we succeed in what He wants us to do. He is the same yesterday, today, and forever. As He taught Moses, He will also teach you what you will say and what you will do. Surely, you will succeed in that assignment because God will teach you to succeed in it.

Divine Impact

God's presence enables us to make the necessary impact in His purpose. Apostle Paul said, *"But the Lord stood with me and strengthened me, so that the message might be preached fully through me, and that all the Gentiles might hear. And I was delivered out of the mouth of the lion. 2 Timothy 4:17.* David encouraged Solomon to build the temple according to the pattern given by God. 1 Chronicles 28:20-21 says, *"And David said to his son Solomon, 'Be strong and of good courage, and do it; do not fear nor be dismayed, for the LORD God; my God; will be with you. He will not leave you nor forsake you, until you have finished all the work for the service of the house of the LORD. "Here are the divisions of the priests and the Levites for all the service of the house of God; and every willing craftsman will be with you for all manner of workmanship, for every kind of service; also the leaders and all the people will be completely at your command."* These are examples for us. God invests in us so that we can make an impact in fulfilling His purpose. The Lord's desire is for us to accomplish the assignment He gives us. We make an impact only when the assignment is successfully completed. It is for this purpose that God works with us. For example, in Acts 10, while Peter was preaching in the house of Cornelius, Jesus Christ baptized the people with the Holy Spirit. As I was preaching in Boston, Massachusetts, in the year 2001, the Lord did the same thing. Everyone in the church was baptized with the Holy Spirit, and we were filled with joy.

Divine Peace

God enforces peace to those who concentrate on fulfilling His purpose. His presence assures peace. The Lord Jesus said, *"And He who sent Me is with Me. The Father has not left Me alone, for I always do those things that please Him." John 8:29.* In Isaiah 66:12-13, we have this promise: *"For thus says the LORD: "Behold, I will extend peace to her like a river, and the glory of the Gentiles like a flowing stream. Then you shall feed; On her sides shall you be carried, and be dandled on her knees. As one whom his mother comforts, so I will comfort you; And you shall be comforted in Jerusalem."* To His disciples, and by extension to us, Jesus said, *"Peace I leave with you, My peace I give to you; not as the world gives do I give to you. Let not your heart be troubled, neither let it be afraid." John 14:27.* He promised an abundance of peace to the righteous. Psalm 72:7 says, *"In His days the righteous shall flourish, and abundance of peace, until the moon is no more."* God will grant us peace if we choose to fulfill His purpose because 1 Thessalonians 3:16 says, *"Now the Lord of peace give you peace always by all means. The Lord be with you all."* Peace is guaranteed to those who commit to His purpose because it is essential for fulfilling purpose.

Divine Help
Divine help is available to those who desire to fulfill the purpose of God. God always works all things according to the counsel of His own will - Ephesians 1:11. He helps those who embrace and diligently work for His purpose. Those who refuse the purpose of God deny themselves divine help. Those who desire to fulfill the purpose of God but rely on their own abilities forfeit divine help. We cannot fulfill the will of God in our own strength. In John 15:5, Jesus said, *"Without me you can do nothing."* Zechariah 4:6 states that divine assignment cannot be fulfilled by our might or by our power but by the Spirit of God. 1 Samuel 2:9 says, *"By strength shall no man prevail."* Psalm 33:16-17 says, *"There is no king saved by the multitude of an host: a mighty man is not*

delivered by much strength. An horse is a vain thing for safety: neither shall he deliver any by his great strength." Jeremiah 10:23-24 says, *"O LORD, I know that the way of man is not in himself: it is not in man that walketh to direct his steps. O LORD, correct me, but with judgment; not in thine anger, lest thou bring me to nothing."* Ecclesiastes 9:11 says, *"I returned, and saw under the sun, that the race is not to the swift, nor the battle to the strong, neither yet bread to the wise, nor yet riches to men of understanding, nor yet favour to men of skill; but time and chance happeneth to them all."* Anyone attempting to fulfill the purpose of God by his or her skills, strategies, connections, etc., will be a resounding failure.

In John 5:30, Jesus Christ said, *"I can of myself do nothing."* We need the help of God to do anything He purposed for us to do. God's omnipotence is available to everyone who chooses to fulfill His will. He promised to help those who embrace His purpose. Isaiah 41:10-13 says, *"Fear not, for I am with you; Be not dismayed, for I am your God. I will strengthen you, Yes, I will help you, I will uphold you with My righteous right hand.'* *"Behold, all those who were incensed against you shall be ashamed and disgraced; They shall be as nothing, and those who strive with you shall perish. You shall seek them and not find them; Those who contended with you. Those who war against you shall be as nothing, as a nonexistent thing. For I, the LORD your God, will hold your right hand, saying to you, 'Fear not, I will help you.'*

If you embrace His purpose, God is also saying to you:
- *Fear not, I am with you.*
- *Be not dismayed because I am your God.*
- *I will strengthen you.*

77

- *I will help you.*
- *I will uphold you with the right hand of my righteousness.*
- *Those who are incensed against you shall be ashamed and confounded; they shall be as nothing.*
- *Those who strive with you shall perish. You shall look for them and shall not find them.*
- *Even those that contend with you, those that war against you shall be as nothing and as a thing of naught.*
- *I, the LORD your God, will hold your right hand.*
- *Fear not. I will help you.*
- *I will help you, says the LORD, and your Redeemer, the Holy One of Israel.*
- *I will make you a new sharp threshing instrument having teeth.*
- *You shall thresh the mountains and beat them small, and shall make the hills as chaff. You shall fan them, and the wind shall carry them away, and the whirlwind shall scatter them.*
- *You shall rejoice in the LORD and shall glory in the Holy One of Israel.*
- *When you (the poor and needy) seek water and there is none, and your tongue fails for thirst, I, the LORD, will hear you.*
- *I, the God of Israel, will not forsake you.*
- *I will open rivers in high places and fountains in the midst of the valleys.*
- *I will make the wilderness a pool of water and the dry land springs of water.*
- *I will plant in the wilderness the cedar, the shittah tree, and the myrtle, and the oil tree.*
- *I will set in the desert the fir tree, the pine, and the box tree together.*

- *That they may see, know, consider, and understand together that the hand of the LORD has done this, and the Holy One of Israel has created it.*

This should make you eager and confident to fulfill His purpose. Embrace the assignment He has for you. Cyrus received this grace. God fulfilled the promises He gave to him in Isaiah 45:1-7. He subdued Babylon, the greatest empire of his time. He released the Jews from bondage to build the temple of God in Jerusalem, thereby fulfilling the purpose of God.

In Jeremiah 1:17-19 God told Jeremiah, *"Thou therefore gird up thy loins, and arise, and speak unto them all that I command thee: be not dismayed at their faces, lest I confound thee before them. For, behold, I have made thee this day a defenced city, and an iron pillar, and brasen walls against the whole land, against the kings of Judah, against the princes thereof, against the priests thereof, and against the people of the land. And they shall fight against thee; but they shall not prevail against thee; for I am with thee, saith the LORD, to deliver thee."* He told Joshua that no one would be able to stand up against him - *Joshua 1:5.* He told Paul, *"Be not afraid, but speak, and hold not thy peace: For I am with thee, and no man shall set on thee to hurt thee: for I have much people in this city." Acts 18:9-10.* In Matthew 28:20 He told us, *"I am with you always."* He is with those who engage in His purpose to help them, and they cannot fail to fulfill His purpose.

The help of God is multidimensional and includes divine presence, instruction, empowerment, vindication, counsel, guidance, defense, provision, and many more. When Saul was seeking to kill him, God sent help to David. Soldiers came from all Israel, even from the tribe of Benjamin, which was the tribe of Saul, to help David. *Then some of the sons of Benjamin and Judah came to David at the stronghold.* [17] *And David went out to meet them, and answered and said to them, "If you have come peaceably to me to help me, my heart will be united with you; but if to betray me to my enemies, since there is no wrong in my hands, may the God of our fathers look and bring judgment."* [18] *Then the Spirit came upon Amasai, chief of the captains, and he said: "We are yours, O David; We are on your side, O son of Jesse! Peace, peace to you, And peace to your helpers! For your God helps you." 1 Chronicles 12:16-18.* We must trust and rely on the help of God to fulfill the purpose of God. Apostle Paul trusted the help of God. He said, *"I can do all things through Christ who strengthens me." Philippians 4:13.*

Many people fail to fulfill the purpose of God because they do not rely on His help. By relying on their own power or the help of others, they invariably block the help of God. Isaiah 31:1 says, *"Woe to them that go down to Egypt for help; and stay on horses, and trust in chariots, because they are many; and in horsemen, because they are very strong; but they look not unto the Holy One of Israel, neither seek the LORD!"* Jeremiah 17:5-8 says, *"Thus saith the LORD; Cursed be the man that trusteth in man, and maketh flesh his arm, and whose heart departeth from the LORD. For he shall be like the heath in the desert, and shall not see when good cometh; but shall inhabit the parched places in the wilderness, in a salt land and not inhabited. Blessed is the man that trusteth in the LORD, and whose hope the LORD is. For he shall be as a tree planted by the waters, and that spreadeth out her roots by the river, and shall not see when heat cometh, but her leaf shall be green; and shall not be careful in the year of drought, neither shall cease from yielding fruit."* What determines success or failure in the purpose of God is whom you trust - God or yourself?

God will neither share His glory with another nor His praise with graven images - Isaiah 42:8. For this reason, He frustrates those who do not rely on Him. Psalm 20:7-8 says, *"Some trust in chariots, and some in horses: but we will remember the name of the LORD our God. They are brought down and fallen: but we are risen, and stand upright.* Pride leads to failure. Micah 5:10 says, *"And it shall come to pass in that day, saith the LORD, that I will cut off thy horses out of the midst of thee, and I will destroy thy chariots."* God frustrates the wisdom of the proud. *"For it is written, I will destroy the wisdom of the wise, and will bring to nothing the understanding of the prudent." 1 Corinthians 1:19.* God's help is in His everlasting arm. Psalm 37:40 says, *"And the LORD shall help them and deliver them; He shall deliver them from the wicked, and save them, because they trust in Him."* Trust in the help of God. Hebrews 13:5-6 says, *"Let your conduct be without covetousness; be content with such things as you have. For He Himself has said, "I will never leave you nor forsake you." So we may boldly say: "The LORD is my helper; I will not fear. What can man do to me?"* God has given us help in the Holy Spirit. At the start of the ministry, the Lord told me that *'ministry can only be done in the power of the Holy Spirit.'* In John 16:7, Jesus Christ said that He would send the Helper. The Holy Spirit is the helper of those who engage in the purpose of God. He is the ever-present help in the time of trouble. He is with us like a mighty warrior to accomplish divine objectives.

Defense And Security
One of the most powerful benefits available to those who choose to fulfill the purpose of God is divine protection

and preservation. God always frustrates those who oppose His purpose. He defends those who engage in His purpose and makes them flourish in it. For example, Isaiah 29:5-8 says, *"Moreover the multitude of your foes shall be like fine dust, And the multitude of the terrible ones Like chaff that passes away; Yes, it shall be in an instant, suddenly. You will be punished by the LORD of hosts with thunder and earthquake and great noise, with storm and tempest and the flame of devouring fire. The multitude of all the nations who fight against Ariel, even all who fight against her and her fortress, and distress her, shall be as a dream of a night vision. It shall even be as when a hungry man dreams, and look--he eats; but he awakes, and his soul is still empty; Or as when a thirsty man dreams, and look--he drinks; but he awakes, and indeed he is faint, and his soul still craves: So the multitude of all the nations shall be, who fight against Mount Zion."* No one can successfully hinder or frustrate a person walking in the purpose of God. They are like the wind that cannot be stopped.

God defends those who walk in His purpose. He protected Abraham when Pharaoh took his wife - Genesis 12:10-20. He protected Jacob from Laban - Genesis 31:22-24. God defended David and frustrated Saul's efforts to hunt him down. He defended Daniel against the conspiracy of the ministers of Dairus - Daniel 6. He defended Israel against their enemies. Psalm 105:13-15 says, *"When they went from one nation to another, from one kingdom to another people, He permitted no one to do them wrong; Yes, He rebuked kings for their sakes, saying, "Do not touch My anointed ones, And do My prophets no harm."* He assured, *"I am with you always to the very end of the age." - Matthew 28:20.* He said, *"I will be a wall of fire around her and the glory within." - Zechariah 2:5.* He promised, *"I will not leave you nor forsake you."* - *Hebrews 13:5.* Jeremiah 2:3 said, *"Israel was holiness to the LORD, the firstfruits of His increase. All that devour him will offend; disaster will come upon them," says the LORD."* Protection is assured to those who walk in the purpose of God. He destroyed the army of Pharaoh in the Red Sea and protected Israel from destruction. By divine arrangement, God raised Esther and Mordecai in Medo-Persia to protect the Jews from the wickedness of Haman.

When Sennacherib invaded Judah, Hezekiah encouraged the people, saying, *"Be strong and courageous, be not afraid nor dismayed for the king of Assyria, nor for all the multitude that is with him: for there be more with us than with him: With him is an arm of flesh; but with us is the LORD our God to help us, and to fight our battles. And the people rested themselves upon the words of Hezekiah king of Judah." 2 Chronicles 32:7-8.* God defended them from the king of Assyria. 2 Chronicles 32:21-23 says, *"And the LORD sent an angel, which cut off all the mighty men of valour, and the leaders and captains in the camp of the king of Assyria. So he returned with shame of face to his own land. And when he was come into the house of his god, they that came forth of his own bowels slew him there with the sword. Thus the LORD saved Hezekiah and the inhabitants of Jerusalem from the hand of Sennacherib the king of Assyria, and from the hand of all other, and guided them on every side. And many brought gifts unto the LORD to Jerusalem, and presents to Hezekiah king of Judah: so that he was magnified in the sight of all nations from thenceforth."* The Lord still shames those who oppose His purpose. He still destroys them.

You have total security when you are in the purpose of God. You are secure on every side. God preserves you all

83

around because it is written: *"He shall deliver you in six troubles, yes, in seven no evil shall touch you. [20] In famine He shall redeem you from death, and in war from the power of the sword. [21] You shall be hidden from the scourge of the tongue, and you shall not be afraid of destruction when it comes. [22] You shall laugh at destruction and famine, and you shall not be afraid of the beasts of the earth. [23] For you shall have a covenant with the stones of the field, and the beasts of the field shall be at peace with you. [24] You shall know that your tent is in peace; You shall visit your dwelling and find nothing amiss. Job 5:19-24*. If you want to be secure without fear of any evil, enlist yourself in the purpose of God, and He will ensure that no evil befalls you.

The Purpose Of God Is Your Health Insurance
God grants breakthroughs, health, strength, prosperity, victory, honor, favor, and longevity to those who engage in His purpose. Exodus 23:25-27 says, *"And ye shall serve the LORD your God, and he shall bless thy bread, and thy water; and I will take sickness away from the midst of thee. There shall nothing cast their young, nor be barren, in thy land: the number of thy days I will fulfil. I will send my fear before thee, and will destroy all the people to whom thou shalt come, and I will make all thine enemies turn their backs unto thee."* These blessings are assured to you. So long as you give yourself to the purpose of God, you have immunity against satanic attacks on your health. You will live in divine health.

In 1998, after I came to the United States on the Lord's assignment, I was meditating on the mission, and the Lord said to me, *"You are my vehicle. I am the driver. I am the best driver there is. If I take you through a rough place, that is the best place there is. I take care of you so that you don't break down on me."*

84

No Obstruction, Limitation, Or Stagnation
The enemy tries to hinder the purpose of God using many devices, but God always frustrates his schemes. The high priests and the Sadducee locked up the Apostles to stop the preaching of the kingdom of God. In Acts 5:17-20, God sent an angel to release them and to instruct them to preach "all the words of this life." As soon as the ministry took off in Jerusalem, Herod seized James. After killing him, he took Peter also and locked him up, intending to arraign him after the Passover. However, God sent His angel, who brought Peter out of prison and thwarted Herod's plan. Shortly after, an angel of God struck Herod; he was eaten by worms and died - Acts 12:1-24. Paul and Silas were put in prison to hinder the purpose of God, but as they sang and praised God, there was an earthquake. The prison doors were flung open, and the bonds of all prisoners were broken. Paul and Silas were released to continue their ministry - Acts 16:22-26.

If you are in the purpose of God, you can expect Him to make room for you to fulfill it. He will frustrate those who oppose you. He told Joshua that no one would be able to stand up against him. Being the Almighty God and ruler of the universe, God works with us to accomplish His purpose by silencing all opposition. When you are in the will of God, nothing can successfully hinder, obstruct, limit, or stagnate you.

Rewards And Inheritance
God crafted and fitted us for the work He wants us to do. Ephesians 2:10 says, *"For we are His workmanship, created in Christ Jesus for good works, which God prepared beforehand that we should walk in them."* No one struggles to do what God designed him to do. If you embrace the purpose of God, you will never struggle to fulfill it because God has built success into it. God wants

us to accomplish great things. He works in and with us, by the operation of the gifts of grace, to fulfill the purpose He has for us. Ephesians 1:11 says, ***"In whom also we have obtained an inheritance, being predestinated according to the purpose of him who worketh all things after the counsel of his own will:"*** He works all things in favor of those who desire and engage in His purpose.

Every believer has an inheritance in Christ. God gives inheritance according to His purpose. If we live for the purpose of God, we will obtain the inheritance. Those who abandon the purpose of God for their selfish desires forfeit their inheritance. 1 Peter 1:3-5 says, ***"Blessed be the God and Father of our Lord Jesus Christ, which according to his abundant mercy hath begotten us again unto a lively hope by the resurrection of Jesus Christ from the dead, To an inheritance incorruptible, and undefiled, and that fadeth not away, reserved in heaven for you, who are kept by the power of God through faith unto salvation ready to be revealed in the last time."*** In Christ, we have an inheritance that is imperishable and enduring. It cannot diminish in value. It is inexhaustible, and it is preserved in heaven. Economic crises, good or bad government, weather, war, or satanic schemes cannot change it. It is guaranteed to those who fulfill His plan.

We should not be enticed and trapped by the system of this world. The Creator and owner of all things has given us an inheritance in Christ. When He gave the land to the tribes of Israel by lot, no family was left out. Though Zelophehad died in the wilderness, God instructed Moses to give an inheritance to his daughters among their father's tribe - Numbers 27:1-11. Our inheritance in the kingdom of God is real. It is predetermined and cannot go to someone else. It is allocated according to the purpose that God wants to fulfill in us. To receive the inheritance, therefore, you must be in the purpose of God. Being born again is the gateway, but you must engage in the purpose for which you were saved to enjoy the full inheritance.

To obtain the inheritance, we must do what God says we should do. Revelation 22:12 said, *"And behold, I am coming quickly, and my reward is with me, to give to every one according to his work."* The reward is the inheritance given to individuals according to their works. Our work is to do the will of God, and doing what God wants is obedience. Obedience is the only way to fulfill the purpose of God. Jeremiah 7:23-24 says, *"But this thing commanded I them, saying, Obey my voice, and I will be your God, and ye shall be my people: and walk ye in all the ways that I have commanded you, that it may be well unto you. But they hearkened not, nor inclined their ear, but walked in the counsels and in the imagination of their evil heart, and went backward, and not forward."* If we disobey the voice of God, we cannot fulfill His purpose or have progress and success. If we disobey, we will forfeit the inheritance. God works all things according to the counsel of His own will - Ephesians 1:11. He will not support any agenda that is contrary to His purpose.

The Lord illustrated this to me many years ago when He taught me through Isaiah 46:9-11 that He would not answer any prayer that is not centered on His purpose. In that Scripture, the Lord said, *"What I have purposed, that will I do."* This means that he will not do what he has not purposed. Most believers, being ignorant of the pivotal position of God's purpose, set their own agenda. They fast and pray, expecting God to help them achieve their objectives. They forget that God is under no obligation to do so. Jesus Christ taught us to pray that *"Thy will be done on earth as it is in heaven." - Matthew 6:10.* God is committed only to His own purpose. Those who forget this will always struggle, stumble, and fall. They cry, weep, and continue in fruitless efforts, not realizing that all they need to do is submit to the plan of God. By relentlessly going after the dictates of your own mind, you will jeopardize your breakthrough, success, victory, and peace. Jeremiah 7:24 said that because they followed the imagination of their evil hearts, they went backward and not forward. By replacing the plan of God with your own, you will forfeit divine support and suffer unnecessarily.

Anyone who embraces the purpose of God has assurance of success. In Isaiah 46:9-11, He said, *"Remember the former things of old: for I am God, and there is none else; I am God, and there is none like me, declaring the end from the beginning, and from ancient times the things that are not yet done, saying, my counsel shall stand, and I will do all my pleasure: Calling a ravenous bird from the east, the man that executeth my counsel from a far country: yea, I have spoken it, I will also bring it to pass; I have purposed it, I will also do it.* To give us confidence, He directed us to His work in the past. He said, "Remember the former things." The works He did in the past assure us of His capability and competence. He is God, and there is none else. He is God, and there is none like Him. No one can compare with Him. He is the sovereign God. He can do all things. Nothing is hard or impossible for Him.

By declaring the end from the beginning, God establishes the operating principles that will effectuate His desire. Nothing can prevent God from doing what He chose to do. His counsel shall stand. It cannot be hindered. Nothing can prevent the purpose of God from coming to pass. He will do what pleases Him. No one can stop Him. He will accomplish His plan. Isaiah 14:24-26 says, *"The LORD of hosts hath sworn, saying, surely as I have thought, so shall it come to pass; and as I have purposed, so shall it stand."* Nothing can undermine or destroy the plan of God. Embracing the purpose of God will shield us from disappointment, failure, and frustration. It is sensible to be part of what will succeed, which is the purpose of God.

Psalm 78:5-7 says, *"For He established a testimony in Jacob, and appointed a law in Israel, which He commanded our fathers, that they should make them known to their children; that the generation to come might know them, the children who would be born, that they may arise and declare them to their children, that they may set their hope in God, and not forget the works of God, but keep His commandments."* This Scripture identifies four reasons why the word of God, His works (testimonies) and the nature of His relationship with us must be emphasized in the body of Christ. They are to:

- testify to the wonderful works of God.
- stimulate the faith of others in God.
- encourage trust in His counsel and ways.
- motivate obedience to His instructions.

Those who engage in fulfilling the purpose of God will experience these things. Their faith will be stimulated. Their experience of God's kindness will trigger gratitude and thanksgiving. They will draw closer to God, and as they obey His instructions, they will receive the blessing He promised - *Isaiah 1:19; Job 36:5-12.*

We all desire the blessings discussed in this chapter. They are available to all. They are not withheld from any of us because they are the normal experience of those who are devoted to fulfilling the purpose of God. This makes our engagement in the purpose of God beneficial. The purpose of God is powerful because by devoting ourselves to it, we access the blessings. Therefore, if you want to live a life of power, enjoying divine spiritual authority, divine support, the presence of God, angelic assistance, divine provision, divine protection and preservation, divine guidance, divine impact, divine help, defense and security, divine health, continuous progress, inheritance from God, and many more, simply commit to the purpose of God and faithfully fulfill it. You are not saved to struggle through life. Our Father is faithful, compassionate, merciful, and generous towards us. He has a plan that gives you all the blessings you seek and more. Just get in His purpose for your life, and you will wish you had done it earlier.

We are all ministers of God. Locate your place, whether it is in ministering the word of God or in education, finance, business, politics, public service, medicine, engineering, sports, arts, entertainment, government, or any other endeavor that enhances or empowers human productivity, lifestyle, and peace. Devote yourself to it and do it as unto the Lord Jesus Christ with all your heart, with all your soul, and with all your strength. You are created to fulfill the purpose of God.

The purpose of God is the power of God for your life.

Chapter Six

MINDSET FOR FULFILLING PURPOSE

The purpose of God is the assignment He gives us to do. Believers are created in Christ Jesus for good works. The good works are the things that God wants us to do. To do these good works, God commands, channels, and structures all things in our favor. Embracing God's purpose makes all things work together for our good - Romans 8:28.

Two principles must be established in our minds if we want to fulfill the purpose of God. The first is the principle of stewardship, and the second is the principle of humility. We cannot fulfill the purpose of God without the practice of these principles. To access the tremendous power available to those who want to fulfill the purpose of God, we must understand stewardship and humility.

Stewardship

Ignorance continues to rob believers of the limitless blessings available in the kingdom of God. Most believers ignorantly make themselves, rather than Jesus Christ, the central focus of their lives. They desire and seek the blessings of God but do not subscribe to the principle of stewardship, which is the channel for appropriating those blessings. They adopt selfish methods that obstruct and separate them from the blessings that they zealously, desperately, and sincerely seek. Embracing stewardship is the only means to avoid ineffectiveness and frustration.

Who Is A Steward?

A steward is a person who manages the resources and affairs of another person in the manner stipulated by the owner. A steward receives resources from his master, his master's instructions on what to do with the resources, and carries out the instructions exactly as instructed by his master. John 5:36 says, ***"But I have greater witness than that of John: for the works which the Father hath given me to finish, the same works that I do, bear witness of me, that the Father hath sent me."*** The main function of a steward is to actualize the desire of his master, not his own. In John 6:38 Jesus Christ said, ***"For I came down from heaven, not to do mine own will, but the will of him that sent me."*** The steward does not decide what he would do with the resources of his master but uses them as the master instructs. He is only faithful if he obeys his master. Any variation of the master's instruction violates and usurps his master's authority. Genesis 24 is a good example of the ministry and operation of a true steward. Taking instructions and resources from his master, Eliezer went to Syria to accomplish his master's desire. He devoted himself to his mission and prayed for its success. He did not convert or divert his master's resources for personal use. After securing the bride for his master's son, he did not tarry but returned immediately to Canaan.

Dedication to fulfilling the mission is the character of a good steward. The Lord reinforced this to me in the counsel He gave me after calling me into ministry. He said, *"A servant has no plan of his own. His master's plan is his plan."* He also said to me, *"A servant has no word of his own. His master's words are his words."* The paramount responsibility of the steward is to fulfill the wishes of his master. In John 4:24, Jesus Christ said, ***"My meat is to do the will of Him that sent me, and to finish the work."*** A good steward does not subordinate the wishes of his master to his own but faithfully fulfills them.

We Are Stewards

1 Timothy 6:7 says, *"For we brought nothing into this world and it is certain we can carry nothing out."* God created and owns all things. He created and endowed us with unique gifts to fulfill His purpose. He gave us skills, talents, knowledge, understanding, intelligence, and the ability to function - 1 Corinthians 12:28-30 and Romans 12:6-8. He gave us a passion for what He wants us to do. He orders things to give us peace, joy, and fulfillment in what He wants us to do. He gave us Apostles, Prophets, Evangelists, Pastors, and Teachers to equip and train us for the work of ministry - Ephesians 4:8-14. He gave us the Holy Spirit to empower us - Acts 1:8. He gave us the gifts of the Holy Spirit - 1 Corinthians 12:4-11, 1 Peter 4:10 to minister to others. Since God gave us these things, we must use them faithfully as good stewards to fulfill His purpose. In 1 Corinthians 4:1, Apostle Paul said, *"Let a man so account of us, as of the ministers of Christ, and stewards of the mysteries of God."* Unlike many, Paul did not use his gifts for personal gain, but he dedicated himself to the assignment that God gave him.

We brought nothing to the world. God gave us our bodies when He knitted us together in the womb - Psalm 139:14; Jeremiah 1:5; and Hebrews 10:5-7. All that we have, we received to fulfill the purpose of God. God owns us. We do not own ourselves, and all that we claim to own belongs to Him. He owns our life, time, ability, money, and possessions. We must use them to serve Him. We must use our bodies to serve God because they are the temple of God. 1 Corinthians 4:2 says, *"Moreover, it is required in stewards, that a man be found faithful."* We must not use what we have for selfish gain. We must not use our position to oppress but must stand for what is true,

93

just, and right. If we do not use what God gave us for His purpose, we will fail in our stewardship - Luke 12:42-48.

Not only did Apostle Paul admonish us to faithfully fulfill our stewardship, but he also did the same. In Philippians 3:13-14 he said, *"..this one thing I do, forgetting those things which are behind, and reaching forth unto those things which are before, I press toward the mark for the prize of the high calling of God in Christ Jesus."* Using his own example, he told Timothy and us by extension, *"..watch thou in all things, endure afflictions, do the work of an evangelist, make full proof of thy ministry. For I am now ready to be offered, and the time of my departure is at hand. I have fought a good fight, I have finished my course, I have kept the faith" 2 Timothy 4:5-7.* Like Paul, we must fight the good fight of faith and faithfully finish our assignment. We must follow David's example of whom it was said: *"He chose David also his servant, and took him from the sheepfolds: From following the ewes great with young he brought him to feed Jacob his people, and Israel his inheritance. So he fed them according to the integrity of his heart; and guided them by the skillfulness of his hands." Psalm 78:70-72.* With integrity of heart, we must use what God gives us to fulfill His purpose on earth.

Paul vouched for Timothy, saying, *"For I trust in the Lord Jesus to send Timothy to you shortly, that I also may be encouraged when I know you state. For I have no one like-minded, who will sincerely care for your state. For all seek their own, not the things which are of Christ Jesus."* Philippians 2:19-21. This is a testimony all of us who desire to serve the Lord Jesus must embrace. Paul said that all seek their own and not the things of Christ Jesus. A good steward does not allow personal desire to disrupt his dedication to his master. We must devote our lives to the Lord Jesus in all sincerity and with integrity of heart, as a demonstration of our gratitude for all that He has done for us.

Our Stewardship Is To Fulfill The Purpose Of God

To be faithful stewards of God, we must fulfill the ministry He gave us - Colossians 4:17. God has a purpose for everyone - Jeremiah 1:5. He created and endowed us to fulfill His purpose. The purpose is our destiny. It is our ministry. It is our stewardship. It is the reason for which we live. Correct teaching of the word of God should eliminate ignorance, highlight the central position of the purpose of God, and encourage dedication to fulfilling it. We should discourage people from living as if God has no plan for their lives. God works all things in us, for us, with us, and through us to fulfill His purpose - Jeremiah 1:5-10, 29:11, Zechariah 8:15 and Isaiah 46:4. People generally use the mind, ability, and resources that God gave them to pursue selfish goals rather than the purpose of God. Deuteronomy 11:10-12 says, *"For the land which you go to possess is not like the land of Egypt from which you have come, where you sowed your seed and watered it by foot, as a vegetable garden; "but the land which you cross over to possess is a land of hills and valleys, which drinks water from the rain of heaven, "a land for which the LORD your God cares; the eyes of the LORD your God are always on it, from the beginning of the year to the very end of the year."* To fulfill the purpose for which God created and saved us, we must learn and practice what pleases Him. We must embrace the change of attitude and lifestyle He requires.

The Purpose Of God Is A Gift To Us

The purpose for which God created you is a gift to you. Numbers 18:7 said, *"Therefore you and your sons with you shall attend to your priesthood for everything at the*

95

altar and behind the veil; and you shall serve. I give your priesthood to you as a gift for service, but the outsider who comes near shall be put to death." The Levites had all their needs met in the service of the Lord. They were preserved, blessed, and honored. Revelation 5:9-10 says, *"And they sang a new song, saying: "You are worthy to take the scroll and open its seals; For you were slain and have redeemed us to God by your blood out of every tribe and tongue and people and nation, And have made us kings and priests to our God; And we shall reign on the earth."* As kings and priests, we have access to enormous spiritual and divine blessings if we engage in the purpose of God. This is the reason that God:

- Created us
- Saved us, and
- Called us in Christ.

Humility

The second most important thing required for fulfilling the purpose of God is humility. We received all that we have from God and must use it to fulfill His purpose. Gifts differ from one person to another. Some have more than others. In Matthew 25:14-15, Jesus taught, *"For the kingdom of heaven is like a man traveling to a far country, who called his own servants and delivered his goods to them. And to one he gave five talents, to another two, and to another one, to each according to his own ability; and immediately he went on a journey."* Those who have more should be humble, and those who have less should be diligent. We must humbly use our gifts for the purpose of God. 1 Corinthians 12:12-30 says that as each part of our body functions in the body, so are we to function in the body of Christ.

Those who feel important need others. In humility, we must appreciate the roles of others. Interdependence is needed to fulfill the purpose of God. Paul planted, Apollo watered, and God gave the increase - 1 Corinthians 3:6. Romans 12:3-6 says, *"For I say, through the grace given to me, to everyone who is among you, not to think of himself more highly than he ought to think, but to think soberly, as God has dealt to each one a measure of faith. For as we have many members in one body, but all the members do not have the same function, so we, being many, are one body in Christ, and individually members of one another. Having then gifts differing according to the grace that is given to us, let us use them: if prophecy, let us prophesy in proportion to our faith."* We must neither feel inferior nor superior but serve God with the gifts that He gave us.

Romans 11:20 states that we should not be high-minded. As 1 Timothy 6:7 told us, we brought nothing into the world and will take nothing out of it. We received what we have and should not be blinded by it - 1 Corinthians 4:7. We must use it in the service of the Lord - 1 Peter 4:8. The Lord Jesus Christ said in Matthew 23:11-12 that he who will be the greatest among us shall be the servant and that God humbles those who exalt themselves and exalts those who humble themselves. Disobedience is indicative of pride, and it brings downfall, as was the case with Saul, the first king of Israel - 1 Samuel 15. It encourages abuse of office, as was the case with Haman, who plotted to destroy the people of God - Esther 3. It breeds callousness, as was the case with Rehoboam, the son of Solomon, who did not respond to the needs of the people of Israel but mocked them - 1 Kings 12. God humbled all of them. Saul lost the throne to David, Haman lost his position to Mordecai, and Rehoboam lost ten tribes to Jeroboam.

The Scriptures say, *"The fear of the LORD is to hate evil: pride, and arrogancy, and the evil way, and the froward mouth, do I hate."* - Proverbs 8:13. *"When pride cometh, then cometh shame: but with the lowly is wisdom."* - Proverbs 11:2. Proverbs 13:10 says, *"Only by pride cometh contention: but with the well advised is wisdom."* Proverbs 16:18 says, *"Pride goes before destruction, and a haughty spirit before a fall."* Pride also causes deception because Obadiah 1:3 says, *"the pride of thine heart hath deceived thee."* Proverbs 29:23 says, *"A man's pride shall bring him low: but honour shall uphold the humble in spirit."* God promotes the humble. He gives grace to the humble - Proverbs 3:34. When we humble ourselves before God, He lifts us up - James 4:10 and 1 Peter 5:6. When Jesus Christ humbled Himself to fulfill the plan of God, He was exalted - Philippians 2:5-11 If we also humble ourselves to fulfill the plan of God, we will receive His approval.

Pursuing The Purpose Of God Is Safe
Before investing in an economy, investors do research to determine effective demand, investment climate, rate of return, stability, profit repatriation policy, and mobility of investment in the economy. Usually, all other things being equal, they invest where the average rate of return is high, expecting a yield that is at least equal to or higher than the average rate of return in the economy. Jesus Christ said, *"Do not lay up for yourselves treasures on earth, where moth and rust destroy and where thieves break in and steal; 20 but lay up for yourselves treasures in heaven, where neither moth nor rust destroys and where thieves do not break in and steal. 21 For where your treasure is, there your heart will be also." Matthew 6:19-21.* Jesus Christ assured us that there is no loss in the economy of heaven. It is far better than the economy of the world. Our

investment is safe in the economy of heaven. If you invest in a safe economy, you will have peace. Investors carefully monitor the economy, and when they perceive economic or political instability, they move their investments elsewhere. They have peace when their investments are safe. Applying yourself to seeking the kingdom of God and His righteousness is investing in the economy of the kingdom of God. The economy of the kingdom is the economy of heaven. It is profitable and safe. You can invest all your treasures in it.

Great success awaits those who invest in the kingdom of God. Jesus Christ, describing the kingdom, said, *"To what shall we liken the kingdom of God? Or with what parable shall we picture it? ^{31} It is like a mustard seed which, when it is sown on the ground, is smaller than all the seeds on earth; ^{32} but when it is sown, it grows up and becomes greater than all herbs, and shoots out large branches, so that the birds of the air may nest under its shade." Mark 4:30-32.* Looking at this in economic terms, the smallest investment in the kingdom of God will yield a great reward. The average rate of return is far higher than in the earthly economy. Job 8:7 says, *"Though your beginning was small, yet your latter end would increase abundantly."* Ecclesiastes 7:8a says, *"The end of a thing is better than its beginning."* For the end of a thing to be better than its beginning, there must be continuous improvement. Proverbs 4:18 also says, *"But the path of the just is like the shining sun, that shines ever brighter unto the perfect day."* There is increasing productivity, impact, and accomplishment for those who responsibly accept their godly purpose and calling.

God always starts great things small. From two people (Adam and Eve) the population of the world has grown to more than seven billion. God made Abraham and Sarah the father and mother of many nations, even though they did not have a child until their old age. Jesus Christ will reign forever on the throne of David, who answered the call of God when he was a shepherd boy and became the king of Israel. Samuel, who was brought to Shiloh to serve God just after his mother weaned him from the breast, became a great prophet. God uses small things to do mighty things. He raises the downtrodden, makes fools competent, and their success glorifies Him.

Your failure will not glorify God. God created things to succeed. He created the seed to succeed. In every seed is a fruit-bearing tree. A seed planted in the right place at the right time does not fail. God built success into our assignment just as He did into the seed. He created us to be successful in the assignment that He gives us. If we embrace our assignment in the place and at the time that He chooses, using the gifts that He gives us, working in the power of the Holy Spirit, and being led by the Holy Spirit, we will succeed. You cannot fail in the assignment that God gives you.

Lessons From Jesus Christ
Jesus Christ, through His ministry, taught us the following:
    1. **Dedication.**
The dictionary defines dedication as the act of binding oneself to a course of action. It is allegiance, commitment, and loyalty. It is complete and wholehearted fidelity. As Christ was totally committed to our salvation, we must be totally committed and dedicate ourselves to fulfilling the purpose of God - John 6:38; 1 Peter 4:1-2.

    2. **Tenacity.**
This means persistent determination, perseverance, and persuasion. The commitment of the Lord was so strong that no obstacle, criticism, betrayal, or pain discouraged

Him. We also must persevere to fulfill the purpose of God - John 12:27-29; Matthew 26:52-54; 2 Peter 3:10-14.

3. Humility.
Humility is the lack of false pride - John 5:19, 30; 4:34. James 4:10 and 1 Peter 5:5-6 encourage humility and submission to God. Romans 12:3 says, *"For I say, through the grace given unto me, to every man that is among you, not to think of himself more highly than he ought to think; but to think soberly."*

4. Sacrifice
Jesus lacked nothing in heaven, and coming to the earth added nothing to Him. His coming was a great sacrifice, and so was His death that brought redemption to mankind. We must not be selfish but sacrificially serve the Lord as an extension of our love for Him - Philippians 2:5-11.

5. Adaptation.
This means adapting to or making adjustments regarding something. As Jesus Christ adjusted to the condition of life on Earth, so must we make the adjustments necessary to fulfill the purpose that God has for us - Luke 22:27.

6. Contentment,
Contentment is being happy with one's situation in life - 1 Timothy 6:6-7. Contented people do not grumble or complain but happily embrace the tasks that God gives them. This was what our Lord Jesus Christ did. He never once complained but dutifully attended to the purpose of His coming to the world.

7. Pleasure
We must be pleased to pursue and fulfill the purpose of God. Jesus Christ said that His food was to do the work of God and to finish it - John 4:34. This too must be our own

food. We must not regard ministry as a burden. We must fulfill it with pleasure.

We must not put obstacles in the way of other people. We must not discourage them. We must support the work of the Lord. We must build and not destroy. In love, we must minister the grace that God gives us to those who need it. 1 John 4:19-5:2 says, *"We love Him because He first loved us. ²⁰ If someone says, "I love God," and hates his brother, he is a liar; for he who does not love his brother whom he has seen, how can he love God whom he has not seen? ²¹ And this commandment we have from Him: that he who loves God must love his brother also. Whoever believes that Jesus is the Christ is born of God, and everyone who loves Him who begot also loves him who is begotten of Him. ² By this we know that we love the children of God, when we love God and keep His commandments."*

Charity must begin at home. It must begin in the church. We cannot impact others until we impact one another.
- We must make our wisdom, skills, and resources available to benefit one another.
- We must lift up those who are down in our midst.
- We must motivate and help one another.
- We must discourage isolation.
- We must not avoid the company of one another.
- We must bind ourselves together in the love of Christ and discourage things that hurt or divide us.
- We must engage our strength and improve our weaknesses so as to be fruitful in our service.

In summary, to fulfill the purpose of God, you must:
- Know the Lord - Be born again.
- Know the word of God.

- Know the specific purpose of God for your life.
- Know the specific place of your assignment.
- Know and minister to the people God sends you to.
- Have faith - 2 Timothy 4:7.
- Be led by the Holy Spirit - Acts 8; 10; 17.
- Be passionate - Proverbs 22:29; Hebrews 6:11-12.
- Persevere and make the sacrifices demanded.
- Develop the fruit of the Holy Spirit - Galatians 5:22-23.
- Engage the gifts of the Holy Spirit - 1 Corinthians 12:7-10; 1 Peter 4:10; 1 Timothy 6:17-19; Romans 12:6-8.
- Walk in love - 1 John 4:7-11; 1 Corinthians 13.
- Be content - 1 Timothy 6:3-6.
- Fast and pray - Ephesians 6:18; 1 Thessalonians 5:17, 25; Luke 18:1; Philippians 4:6-7.
- Put on the whole armor of God - Ephesians 6:10-17; 2 Peter 1:5-9.
- Avoid distractions.

God created and called us for His glory. All that we do must honor Him. Malachi 2:1-3 says, *"And now, O priests, this commandment is for you. If you will not hear, and if you will not take it to heart, to give glory to My name," says the LORD of hosts, "I will send a curse upon you, and I will curse your blessings. Yes, I have cursed them already, because you do not take it to heart. Behold, I will rebuke your descendants and spread refuse on your faces, the refuse of your solemn feasts; and one will take you away with it."* We honor God when we diligently use the grace invested in us for the blessing of others. Jesus Christ said, *"I do not seek my own will but the will of the Father who sent me." John 5:30.* Your position in life is determined by how much of the grace of God you release to honor His name. When you selflessly and zealously use the gifts that God has given you to be a blessing to others, God will release heavenly blessings upon you. If you do not serve God with what He gave you, your blessing is cursed. This is the root cause of the struggles most believers go through in life. Hebrews 6:1-4.

Remember that you are a steward because God gave you everything you have. You brought nothing into the world. You possess everything you have by the grace of God. God gave you your race, color, intelligence, strength, sex, physique, job, business, family, relationships, connections, and friends. Without God, you are nothing, and without Him, you can do nothing. Embracing this truth in humility will transform your mind, produce gratitude in you, and equip you to be a faithful steward of God to fulfill His purpose with all your heart.

WARNING
On January 5, 2003, it was revealed to me in a vision that a church had abandoned its primary purpose of preparing believers for, and making the world aware of, the coming of the Lord. The Church must turn from its devotion to money and other distractions to its main purpose of preparing the saints for the work of ministry.

A great shaking is upon the world. We must turn away from distractions and be fully engaged in seeking the Lord. Our peace depends on this, and so does our impact in this world. Our faith must go beyond mere belief. It must result in action, growth in Christian character, and moral discipline. May the good Lord give us the courage to serve Him to the end in the mighty name of Jesus Christ our Lord.

Chapter Seven

CONSEQUENCES OF REJECTING PURPOSE

There are many lines of thought on our position in the universe. Some suggest that things just happen. Others say that we evolved and that no one made us. Many others believe that God created all things, including human beings. Among these are those who do not believe in eternal life but in endless reincarnation for continuous perfection. Of those who believe in eternal life, there are some who are persuaded that it is through their own effort that they will attain it. They believe that at the end, God will judge them based on the good and evil they have done. If their good outweighs their evil, then God will admit them to heaven. Unfortunately, based on the Holy Bible and inferences from it, the positions taken by these categories of people are dangerous.

Why Are They Dangerous?
They are dangerous because the Bible says:
- The purpose of God is eternal, and it is eternally purposed in Christ - Ephesians 3:11.
- All things were created through Christ - John 1:1-3; Colossians 1:15-16.
- He came in the flesh to suffer for the sins of mankind - Isaiah 53:4-8; 2 Corinthians 5:21; Hebrews 2:10.
- all have sinned and fall short of the glory of God - Romans 3:23-24.
- Without the shedding of blood, there is no remission of sins - Hebrews 9:22; Leviticus 17:11.
- Christ made atonement for the sins of the whole world - John 1:29; 1 John 1:1-2.
- Redemption is by faith in what Jesus Christ accomplished for us through His blood - Romans

105

3:25; Ephesians 1:7; Colossians 1:12-13; 1 John 1:7; Revelation 1:5.

- He is eternal life - 1 John 5:11-12.
- He is the only way - John 14:6 i.e., the narrow gate to God.
- He has offered eternal life to all - John 3:16-17; 5:24.
- He will not cast away anyone who comes to Him - John 6:37; Romans 10:12-13.
- By Him all things consist - Colossians 1:17.
- He is the heir of all things - Hebrews 1:2; John 13:3.
- Through Him we become heirs of God - Galatians 4:7; Romans 8:17.
- He is the King of the kingdom of God - Isaiah 9:6-7; Revelations 19:16.
- He is the One who will judge the world - Psalm 96:11; 98:9; Acts 17:31.
- Redemption is available to all through Him only.

Jesus Christ Is The Nobleman
He said therefore, A certain nobleman went into a far country to receive for himself a kingdom, and to return. And he called his ten servants, and delivered them ten pounds, and said unto them, Occupy till I come. But his citizens hated him, and sent a message after him, saying, We will not have this man to reign over us. And it came to pass, that when he was returned, having received the kingdom, then he commanded these servants to be called unto him, to whom he had given the money, that he might know how much every man had gained by trading. Then came the first, saying, Lord, thy pound hath gained ten pounds. And he said unto him, Well, thou good servant: because thou hast been faithful in a very little, have thou authority over ten cities. And the second came, saying, Lord, thy pound hath gained five pounds. And he said likewise to him, Be thou also over five cities.

And another came, saying, Lord, behold, here is thy pound, which I have kept laid up in a napkin: For I feared thee, because thou art an austere man: thou takest up that thou layedst not down, and reapest that thou didst not sow. And he saith unto him, Out of thine own mouth will I judge thee, thou wicked servant. Thou knewest that I was an austere man, taking up that I laid not down, and reaping that I did not sow: Wherefore then gavest not thou my money into the bank, that at my coming I might have required mine own with usury? And he said unto them that stood by, Take from him the pound, and give it to him that hath ten pounds. (And they said unto him, Lord, he hath ten pounds.) For I say unto you, That unto every one which hath shall be given; and from him that hath not, even that he hath shall be taken away from him. But those mine enemies, which would not that I should reign over them, bring hither, and slay them before me. Luke 19:12-27. Jesus Christ, the nobleman, has gone to receive the kingdom and will come back to reign. He will come to judge:

- those who reject Him - Luke 19:27; 1 Peter 4:17; 2 Thessalonians 1:8; Hebrews 6:4-8.
- those who rely on their own goodness and works for salvation - Revelation 20:11-15.
- those living in sin - Revelation 21:8, 27; 22:14-15; Ephesians 5:5; 1 Corinthians 6:9-10: Galatians 5:19-25.
- those who are selfish and do not walk in love - Luke 16:19-31; Matthew 25:31-46.
- the unforgiving - Matthew 6:15; 1 John 1:7-11.

That the kingdom of God is the purpose for creation is evident. Since God has determined and cannot change how His kingdom works, how people will enter into it, and the conduct accepted in it, by ignoring His determined counsel, you exclude yourself from His kingdom. Since no other kingdom will exist and since God will not create another kingdom for those who refuse His counsel, you must consider critically where you will end up. The only way you can be right is if the Holy Bible is wrong, meaning there is no God, or that the Holy Bible does not reflect His desire, counsel, and will. What is going on in the world confirms the Holy Bible. Creation is still speaking of its Creator - Psalm 19. With creation and events unfolding in the world, it is dangerous for you to ignore the truth. I make a personal appeal to you to receive Jesus Christ as your Lord and Savior, embrace His purpose for your life, and live your life based on His counsel and wisdom.

I appeal to you for this reason: I was born and brought up in a Muslim home. Though I did not practice the religion in my youth, I decided to fully embrace the faith when, at the height of my career, I suddenly began to feel that my life was empty and meaningless. I was a professional accountant - a member of the Chartered Institute of Management Accountants. I had an MBA in 1985 and graduated from Manchester Business School - International Bankers Course in 1991. I had a career in industry, management consulting at KPMG, and was a Deputy General Manager at a merchant bank. I was financially established and blessed with a wonderful family. I had what I had always wanted and what many are looking for, but it seemed meaningless. I felt that there must be more to life than what I had lived for. Desperately seeking a way out, I got deeper into voodoo. I knew nothing about Christianity or how the Lord relates to people, but on my way to the voodoo priests, I started having the presence of the Lord in the passenger seat of my car. Though I did not see Him, I knew He was there, and He always engaged me in a dialogue that went like this:

The Lord: You are very hardworking.

Me: Yes

The Lord: You are very successful.

Me: Yes

The Lord: But you have no peace.

Me: (Mute) because I knew it was true.

The Lord: Give your life to Christ, and you will have peace.

This experience went on for months. I could neither stop nor wish it away. It always occurred when I was on my way to voodoo priests for divination and rituals. It did not stop until I decided to accept His counsel. I am amazed at the grace of God in drawing me to Himself and what He has done in my life since that day. If you get hold of my book *'From Muslim and Occultism to Bishop'* and or *'The Wonderful Works of God,'* you will read of some of the wonders that God is capable of. He can do the same and even greater things with you. God is unlimited.

Receive Jesus Christ and His purpose for your life today. Snatch yourself from Satan, who blinds the hearts of men to the Gospel. 2 Corinthians 4:3-5 says, ***"But if our gospel be hid, it is hid to them that are lost: In whom the god of this world hath blinded the minds of them which believe not, lest the light of the glorious gospel of Christ, who is the image of God, should shine unto them. For we preach not ourselves, but Christ Jesus the Lord; and ourselves your servants for Jesus' sake."*** Take the Lord's counsel. ***The law and the prophets were until John: since that time the kingdom of God is preached, and*** *every man presseth into it. Luke 16:16.* Press into the kingdom of God because if you do, you will not regret it.

The power of God is abundantly available to you if you choose to fulfill the purpose of God. You will never be weak or fail, but live your life in the power of the Almighty God. You will be preserved and fulfilled.

OTHER BOOKS BY THE AUTHOR

From Muslim and Occultism to Bishop
God Is The Master Builder
The Work of Life
Understanding Kingdom Economy
Principles of Divine Promotion
The New Covenant Priest
You Have Been Delivered
Understanding The Purpose of God
Knowing and Fulfilling the Purpose of God
Overcoming The Trials of Life
The Wonderful Works of God

About the Author

Femi Owoyemi was born into a Muslim family. He graduated as a Chartered Management Accountant (Prize Winner) at South West London College in 1977. He earned an MBA with distinction from the University of Lagos in 1985 and attended the Manchester Business School - Senior International Bankers Program in 1991. He is a member of the Institute of Chartered Accountants and the Institute of Management Consultants, both in Nigeria.

He was a Financial Management Consultant at KPMG. He joined First City Merchant Bank in 1989 as a Senior Manager and rose to the position of Deputy General Manager in 1992.

Femi Owoyemi became born again through a divine encounter in 1992. He attended the Word of Faith Bible Institute (WOFBI) - June 1996, holds an Associate degree in Theology from the Evangelical Theological College of West Africa in 2003, and a Post Graduate Diploma in Theology from the Redeemed Christian Bible College in 2003. He was awarded an honorary doctorate in Theology from the Evangelical Theological College of West Africa in 2012.

He was ordained an Evangelist in Christ Miracle Vineyard Church in 1994, Pastor in 1998, and District Superintendent (North American Missions) in 2001. He planted two branches of Christ Miracle Vineyard Church in the United States, one in Providence, RI, in 1998 and the other in Boston, MA, in 2000.

In 2010, the Lord called him to establish Kingdom Lighthouse Church in Providence, RI. He has preached extensively and held several outdoor crusades/revivals in Nigeria and the United States. He is married to Pastor Modupe Owoyemi, an attorney, and they are blessed with many children.

www.ingramcontent.com/pod-product-compliance
Lightning Source LLC
LaVergne TN
LVHW041230080426
835508LV00011B/1145

9 781733 233064